NIGHT

Elie Wiesel

AUTHORED by Lindsay Grant
UPDATED AND REVISED by Gemma Cooper-Novack

COVER DESIGN by Table XI Partners LLC
COVER PHOTO by Olivia Verma and © 2005 GradeSaver, LLC

BOOK DESIGN by Table XI Partners LLC

Published by GradeSaver LLC, www.gradesaver.com

First published in the United States of America by GradeSaver LLC. 2015

GRADESAVER, the GradeSaver logo and the phrase "Getting you the grade since 1999" are registered trademarks of GradeSaver, LLC

ISBN 978-1-60259-491-3

Printed in the United States of America

For other products and additional information please visit http://www.gradesaver.com

Table of Contents

Biography of Elie Wiesel (1928–)

Elie Wiesel was born in Sighet, Transylvania on September 30, 1928. He had two older sisters and a younger sister named Tzipora. The town of Sighet is located in present-day Romania, although historically the area has been claimed by the people of both Hungary and Romania. Elie (short for Eliezer) grew up speaking Yiddish at home, and Hungarian, Romanian, and German outside. He also learned classical Hebrew at school. Elie's mother's family was part of the Hasidic sect of Judaism, and Elie loved the mysticism and folk tales of the sect as a child. He devoted the early years of his life to religious studies although his father encouraged him to study modern Hebrew and secular subjects also.

During the early years of World War II, Sighet remained relatively unaffected by the war. Although Sighet became controlled by the Hungarians instead of the Romanians, the Jews in Sighet believed that they would be safe from the persecution that Jews in Germany and Poland were suffering. In 1944, however, Elie and all the other Jews in the town were deported to concentration camps in Poland. Elie and his father were taken to Auschwitz, where they became separated from Elie's mother and younger sister Tzipora. Elie, who was fifteen at the time, never saw them again.

During the following year, Elie was moved to the concentration camps at Buna, Gleiwitz, and Buchenwald. He managed to stay with his father the entire time until his father's death from dysentery, starvation, exposure, and exhaustion at Buchenwald. Finally, in April 1945, Elie was liberated from Buchenwald by the United States Third Army.

After the war, Elie learned that his mother and younger sister had died in the gas chambers, but that his two older sisters had survived. Elie lived in a French orphanage for a few years and in 1948 began to study literature, philosophy, and psychology at the Sorbonne in Paris. He supported himself as a choirmaster and teacher of Hebrew, and he became a journalist, writing for the French newspaper L'Arche and the Israeli Yediot Ahronot. Elie had vowed never to write about his Holocaust experiences, but in 1955, after meeting the French Catholic novelist and Nobel laureate Francois Mauriac, he decided to write And the World Remained Silent, a 900-page volume. The book was originally written in Yiddish and published in Buenos Aires, Argentina. After two years, it appeared again in a compressed, 127-page French version called La Nuit (Night).

In 1956 Elie Wiesel was hit by a taxicab in New York and confined to a wheel chair for almost a year. He applied for American citizenship and after recovering from his injuries, continued to live in New York as a feature writer for a Yiddish-language newspaper called the Jewish Daily Forward. He wrote an additional 35 works in French dealing primarily with Judaism and the Holocaust. His novels include L'Aube (Dawn) and Le Jour (The Accident), which are semi-autobiographical works dealing with Holocaust survivors. In La Ville de la Chance (The Town Beyond the Wall),

Wiesel imagines returning to his home town, which he does only after the novel is published.

Wiesel's other novels include The Gates of the Forest, The Oath, The Testament, and The Fifth Son. He has written plays, including Zalmen, or the Madness of God and The Trial of God, and his essays and short stories are collected in the volumes Legends of Our Time, One Generation After, and A Jew Today. In addition, he has written collections of Hasidic tales and Biblical stories, and the English translation of his memoirs was published in 1995 as All Rivers Run to the Sea. Wiesel continues to write in French, but his wife Marion, who he married in 1969 and who also survived the concentration camps, collaborates with him his books' English translations. Wiesel's books on the Holocaust have helped win him an international reputation.

Wiesel became politically involved after learning about the persecution of Soviet Jews in the USSR. He first traveled to the USSR in 1965 and described the situation he observed in the volume The Jews of Silence. He has continued to plead on the behalf of oppressed peoples in the Soviet Union, South Africa, Vietnam, Biafra, and Bangladesh.

Elie Wiesel has lectured at colleges around the country and has been Andrew Mellon Professor of Humanities at Boston University since 1976. In 1978 he was appointed Chairman of the United States Holocaust Memorial Council by President Jimmy Carter, and in 1985 he was awarded the Congressional Gold Medal of Achievement by President Ronald Reagan. In 1986 Wiesel received the Nobel Prize for Peace. Currently, Elie Wiesel lives in New York City with his wife and son Elisha.

Teacher Guide - About the Author

Eliezer "Elie" Wiesel was born in Sighet, Transylvania (present-day Romania), on September 30, 1928. He had two older sisters, Bea and Hilda, and a younger sister, Tzipora. His parents ran a store in Sighet. Wiesel grew up speaking Yiddish at home and Hungarian, Romanian, and German outside of his home. He also learned classical Hebrew in school. Elie's mother's family was part of the Hasidic sect of Judaism. As a child, Elie was fascinated with the mystical tradition of Kabbalah. He devoted his early years to religious study, though his father encouraged him to study modern Hebrew and secular subjects also.

During the early years of World War II, Sighet remained relatively unaffected by the war. Although the town became controlled by the Hungarians instead of the Romanians, the Jews in Sighet believed they would be safe from the persecution that Jews in Germany and Poland were suffering. However, in 1944, Elie and all the other Jews in Sighet were deported to concentration camps in Poland. Elie and his father were taken to Auschwitz, where they became separated from Elie's mother and younger sister Tzipora. Elie, who was fifteen at the time, never saw them again. During the following year, Elie and his father were moved to the camps at Buna, Gleiwitz, and Buchenwald. The two managed to stay together until his father's death from dysentery, starvation, exposure, and exhaustion at Buchenwald. In April 1945, Elie was liberated from Buchenwald by the United States Third Army.

After the war, Elie lived in a French orphanage for a few years. He learned that his mother and younger sister had died in the gas chambers, but that his two older sisters had survived the war. In 1948 he began to study literature, philosophy, and psychology at the Sorbonne in Paris. He supported himself as a choirmaster and Hebrew teacher before becoming a journalist writing for French newspaper *L'Arche* and the Israeli *Yediot Ahronot*. Wiesel had vowed never to write about his Holocaust experiences; however, in 1955, after meeting the French Catholic novelist and Nobel Laureate Francois Mauriac, he decided to write *And the World Remained Silent*. The 900-page volume was originally written in Yiddish and published in Buenos Aires, Agentina. Two years later, the book was released in a compressed, 127-page French version titled *La Nuit (Night)*.

Wiesel has lectured widely in the United States. He was Distinguished Professor of Judaic Studies at The City University of New York from 1972-1976, and became the Andrew Mellon Professor of Humanities at Boston University in 1976. President Jimmy Carter appointed Wiesel Chairman of the President's Commission on the Holocaust in 1978, and he became Founding Chairman of the United States Holocaust Memorial Council the following year. He has recieved numerous honors and awards, including the Presidential Medal of Freedom, the United States Congressional Gold Medal and the Medal of Liberty Award. In December 1986, Wiesel was awarded the Nobel Prize in Oslo, Norway. With his wife, Marion, Wiesel founded The Elie Wiesel Foundation for Humanity in 1987.

Wiesel has written more than 50 books, which have won many awards.

Biography of Elie Wiesel (1928–)

Teacher Guide - Study Objectives

If all of the elements of this lesson plan are employed, students will develop the following powers, skills, and understanding:

1. If all of the elements of this lesson plan are employed, students will develop the following powers, skills, and understanding:

   1. To process how artists throughout history have represented the Holocaust in a variety of media.

   2. To understand how the events told in *Night* relate to broader historical facts and themes, such as the history of World War II and changing European geography.

   3. To effectively utilize research and presentation tools to create an informational archive and visual timeline of events, figures, and sites related to the novel.

   4. To understand the definition of genocide, and to process how the Holocaust relates to other cases of genocide around the world.

   5. To connect Wiesel's narrative to his larger biography and postwar advocacy efforts.

   6. To read a text carefully with an eye to metaphorical and symbolic language.

   7. To produce sophistocated written and artistic responses to the text and audio-visual materials.

Teacher Guide - Common Core Standards

1. 9-10

   CCSS.ELA-LITERACY.CCRA.R.1
   Read closely to determine what the text says explicitly and to make logical inferences from it; cite specific textual evidence when writing or speaking to support conclusions drawn from the text.

2. 9-10

   CCSS.ELA-LITERACY.CCRA.R.3
   Analyze how and why individuals, events, or ideas develop and interact over the course of a text.

3. 9-10

   CCSS.ELA-LITERACY.CCRA.R.5
   Analyze the structure of texts, including how specific sentences, paragraphs, and larger portions of the text (e.g., a section, chapter, scene, or stanza) relate to each other and the whole.

4. 9-10

   CCSS.ELA-LITERACY.CCRA.R.7
   Integrate and evaluate content presented in diverse media and formats, including visually and quantitatively, as well as in words.

5. 9-10

   CCSS.ELA-LITERACY.CCRA.R.9
   Analyze how two or more texts address similar themes or topics in order to build knowledge or to compare the approaches the authors take.

6. 9-10

   CCSS.ELA-LITERACY.CCRA.W.7
   Conduct short as well as more sustained research projects based on focused questions, demonstrating understanding of the subject under investigation.

7. 9-10

   CCSS.ELA-LITERACY.CCRA.W.8
   Gather relevant information from multiple print and digital sources, assess the credibility and accuracy of each source, and integrate the information while avoiding plagiarism.

8. 9-10

   CCSS.ELA-LITERACY.CCRA.W.9
   Draw evidence from literary or informational texts to support analysis,
   reflection, and research.

9. 9-10

   CCSS.ELA-LITERACY.CCRA.SL.1
   Prepare for and participate effectively in a range of conversations and
   collaborations with diverse partners, building on others' ideas and
   expressing their own clearly and persuasively.

10. 9-10

    CCSS.ELA-LITERACY.CCRA.SL.2
    Integrate and evaluate information presented in diverse media and formats,
    including visually, quantitatively, and orally.

11. 9-10

    CCSS.ELA-LITERACY.CCRA.SL.3
    Evaluate a speaker's point of view, reasoning, and use of evidence and
    rhetoric.

12. 9-10

    CCSS.ELA-LITERACY.CCRA.SL.5
    Make strategic use of digital media and visual displays of data to express
    information and enhance understanding of presentations.

Teacher Guide - Introduction to Night

Night (originally published in French as *La Nuit*) has sold millions of copies and has been published in twenty-five languages since its first printing in 1958. The book tells the story of the young Elie Wiesel, a Hungarian Hasidic Jew and devoted student of the Kabbalah, who in 1944 at the age of fifteen is transported, along with his family, to a series of Nazi-run concentration camps, among them Auschwitz and Buchenwald. Elie and his father (they are separated from his mother and sisters almost immediately, and his mother and youngest sister will not survive the Holocaust) endure unspeakable hardships: abuse, hard labor, starvation, forced marches, and torture. Wiesel portrays the experience in excruciating detail.

Wiesel has said that he struggled to write the book, and after its publication, it took a great deal of time to find its audience. The book was first printed in Argentina in 1956, then edited and translated into French two years later, then re-edited, translated in to English, and published in America in 1960; many publishers thought the material would be too inaccessible or depressing for commercial audiences. However, the book gained readers and traction, and was selling more than 300,000 copies annually in America alone by the mid-nineties. Today, *Night* is often considered the touchstone of Holocaust memoirs, and has been widely read, studied, and distributed. (Oprah Winfrey increased its circulation substantially by selecting it for Oprah's Book Club in 2006.) Because of the book's accessibility and success, Wiesel is considered one of the primary voices of Holocaust survivors.

Night would ultimately become the first of a trilogy; Wiesel published the follow-up volumes *Dawn* in 1960 and *Day* in 1961.

Key Aspects of Night

Tone

The tone of the book is serious and somber, as Wiesel recounts his horrible experiences as a concentration camp prisoner during the Holocaust. The tone is also questioning: Wiesel frequently poses questions provoked by his circumstances that the reader may also contemplate.

Setting

The narrative begins in the village of Sighet, Transylvania (present-day Romania) in 1941, at the height of World War II. Wiesel and his family remain in Sighet until 1944, when they are deported to the Auschwitz-Birkenau concentration camp in Poland. During the train journey to Poland, the deportees stop in Kaschau, a Czechoslovakian border town.

Biography of Elie Wiesel (1928–)

Elie and his father spend three weeks at Auschwitz before being transfered to Buna, one of three camps making up Auschwitz-Birkenau. The majority of the narrative takes place in Buna.

One brief scene is set in postwar Paris, though Wiesel indicates the time only as "many years later."

At the climax of the novel, the prisoners travel from Buna to Gleiwitz on foot, and then from Gleiwitz through Germany by train to the Buchenwald concentration camp. The novel concludes with the liberation of Buchenwald in 1945.

Point of view

The novel is told from a first-person point of view, narrated by Wiesel. Wiesel often breaks into his own narrative to comment retrospectively.

Character development

Elie

At the beginning of the narrative, Elie is thirteen years old and extremely devout in his religious practice. He is attracted to the mystical tradition of Kabbalah, and begins studying with the wayward Moishe the Beadle. The young Elie watches the adults around him react to news from the war front and speculate about their future, but he has little personal control over events. He must quickly adapt to the harsh conditions of life in a concentration camp, where he struggles to stay with his father and to stay alive. During this time, the constant suffering and death all around him harden him emotionally. He struggles with his faith, growing angry at an apparently absent God. He becomes almost singularly focused on food, motivated by his intense and constant hunger. Until the end, he preserves his will to keep his father alive. When his father dies, just before the 1945 liberation of Buchenwald, Elie experiences feelings of remorse for being unable to help his father more in his final moments of life. At the end of the novel, sixteen-year-old Elie is physically transformed in a living "corpse." But it is clear that this physical transformation reflects more permanent emotional and psychological changes. Elie's religious faith and his will to live have been forever compromised, since he will never forget the murder of his mother and three sisters, the death of his father, and the countless horrors he witnessed in the camps.

Elie's father

At the beginning of the book Elie's father has great faith in the world, and dismisses his son's suggestion that the family emigrate. He ignores the magnitude of the impending Nazi invasion. After arriving in the camps, however, he becomes pragmatic and thoughtful. He is both a source of strength for Elie emotionally and a physical burden as he weakens. Near his death, he becomes weak and defenseless.

Akiba Drumer

Over the course of the book, Akiba Drumer loses his faith in God. He becomes "a victim of the selection," and is burned in the crematoria.

Juliek the violinist

Juliek is a resilient character: a committed musician, he has managed to bring his violin with him to the camps, and plays Beethoven in the moments before his death, even though it is prohibited for Jews to play music by German composers.

Themes

Elie's Struggle With His Faith

Elie's struggle to reconcile his belief in God with the atrocities he faces in the concentration camps is a major theme of the novel. At the beginning of the narrative, Elie is extremely devout. The mass murder and brutality he witnesses in the camps, along with the constant fear of his own imminent death, causes Elie to question what was previously a staunch belief in God.

The Will to Survive

Staying alive in the camps is, in large part, a matter of luck; however, it is also a matter of personal resolve. Throughout the novel, Elie's own will to live wavers in the face of starvation, murder, and daily acts of inhumanity. As his faith in God wavers, Elie's connection to his father ultimately maintains his conviction to stay alive. Akiba Drumer falls victim to "selection" when he loses his faith completely, while Rabbi Eliahu's son foresakes his father in his desperate attempt to survive the march to Gleiwitz.

Dehumanization

The dehumanizing effects of the Nazis' bureaucratic system of mass murder take many forms throughout the narrative. First, Elie and his fellow deportees are treated like cattle on the trip from Sighet to Birkenau, crowded into a train car with limited food and water. The Nazis treat their prisoners like animals, killing them and burning their bodies without ceremony. They force Jewish prisoners to work in the crematoria, burning the bodies of their fellow prisoners. The sheer scale and constant rate of the killing necessarily diminishes the emotional impact of each individual death on the living observers. The structural hierarchy of the camp, which places some prisoners in positions of authority over others, engenders violence between prisoners. Furthermore, the constant state of extreme hunger forces prisoners to prioritize food above all else. The desire for food overpowers more subtle emotions, obliterating the prisoners' empathy for one another.

Fathers and Sons

Staying with and protecting his father becomes Elie's primary goal while the two men are in the concentration camps. Without his father present, Elie may have lost the will to live. This bond propels Elie through to the end of the narrative, when his father finally dies in the Buchenwald camp. At times, this relationship puts Elie at risk--in an environment where old age and weakness are grounds for "selection," Elie puts his own life on the line to protect his father's. The relationships between other fathers and sons in the novel, as in that of Rabbi Eliahu and his son, act as foils for Elie's own behavior toward his father.

Symbols

Night

Night signifies death, oblivion, fear, uncertainty, and the strange elasticity of time Elie experiences throughout the novel. After describing the arrival at Auschwitz, Wiesel writes, "Never shall I forget that night, the first night in camp, that turned my life into one long night seven times sealed." Here, night is representative of both the literal time when Elie and his family arrive at the camp, and of the metaphical darkness that envelopes his life during and after the Holocaust. Later, Wiesel asks, "When had we left our homes? And the ghetto? And the train? Only a week ago? One night? *One single night?*" The trauma of deportation and adjusting to life in a concentration camp distorts Wiesel's notion of time; night stands for the all-encompassing horror of these experiences.

Fire

Broadly, fire symbolizes a destructive force more powerful than Elie, his family, his neighbors, and the other prisoners of the concentration camps. At the beginning of the novel, when the Wiesel family--along with the other Jews of Sighet--are speculating about the possibility of deportation, Wiesel writes, "No one was praying for the night to pass quickly. The stars were but sparks of the immense conflagration that was consuming us." This all-consuming represents the inevitability of fate, the uncontrollable forces of the universe. Along these lines, fire often stands for the Nazis' unstoppable campaign of death and destruction. On the train to Auschwitz, a passenger named Mrs. Schächter believes she can see fire outside the train window. Her vision foreshadows the reality of the camps, where prisoners are unceremoiously burned en masse. When Elie and his family arrive at Birkenau, the first thing they see is the fire of the crematoria.

Smoke

Closely related to the symbolic meaning of fire, smoke stands for the death and destruction of the Holocaust. Smoke evokes the mass burning of bodies in the crematoria, which turns Elie's "dreams to ashes."

Silence

Silence symbolizes the lack of God's intervention in the Holocaust--Elie perceives that God has abandoned him and his fellow prisoners in the time of their greatest suffering. It is this silence that causes Elie to question his faith throughout the novel. Furthermore, silence signifies the lack of response and action from the rest of the world, which seems inconceivable to Elie.

Climax

The climactic point of the narrative is the prisoners' nighttime journey on foot from Buna to Gleiwitz. This brutal slog through the snow takes Elie, who has just had an operation on his foot, as close to death as he comes at any other point in the novel. This journey forces the prisoners far beyond the physical capabilities of their malnourished bodies. It is at this point that theme of dehumanization comes to a climax--each prisoner moves like an automaton, tapping into some primal will to survive. As men die along the way, the living prisoners trample them unthinkingly. Hundreds more die after the group arrives in the abandoned town, where Elie tries desperately to keep himself and his father awake in the snow. The theme of father and son relationships also comes to a climactic point here, when Elie compares himself with Rabbi Eliahu's son, who has foresaken his father in the pursuit of his own survival.

Structure

The story is narrated chronologically, with some retrospective digressions by Wiesel. It does not have chapter numbers.

Teacher Guide - Relationship to Other Books

There are countless fictional, nonfictional, and historical works related to the Holocaust; Amazon.com lists 1,373 results for "Holocaust Memoirs" alone. Students will be able to find historical and literary works on almost any aspect of the Holocaust that interests them.

For other reputable first-person accounts of young people during the Holocaust, consider Primo Levi's *Survival in Auschwitz,* Livia Bitton-Jackson's *I Have Lived a Thousand Years: Growing Up in the Holocaust,* Gerda Weissmann Klein's *All But My Life,* Olga Lengyel's *Five Chimneys: The Story of Auschwitz,* Lucille Eichengreen's *From Ashes to Life: My Memories of the Holocaust,* Fanya Gottesfeld Heller's *Love in a World of Sorrow: A Teenage Girl's Holocaust Memoirs,* Dov Freiberg's *To Survive Sobibor, and* Lucy Lipiner's *Long Journey Home: A Young Girl's Memoir of Surviving the Holocaust.*

The two other books in the *Night* trilogy are Wiesel's *Dawn* and *Day.* Other novels featuring adolescents in the Holocaust include Lois Lowry's *Number the Stars*, John Boyne's *The Boy in the Striped Pajamas*, and Anne Holm's *I Am David.*

You may also consider personal narratives from survivors of other genocides, such as Theo Macombe's *The Race For Life: Memoirs of a Rwandan Genocide Survivor*, Immaculee Ilibagiza and Steve Erwin's *Left to Tell: Discovering God Amidst the Rwandan Holocaust*, Chanrithy Him's *Growing Up Under the Khmer Rouge: A Memoir*, Loung Ung's *First They Killed My Father: A Daughter of Cambodia Remembers*, and Grigoris Balakian's *Armenian Golgotha: A Memoir of the Armenian Genocide, 1915-18.*

Teacher Guide - Bringing in Technology

Throughout the study of *Night*, students with particular learning disabilities should have the option of using dictation software for writing assignments, and text-to-speech software for reading assignments.

The long-term activities begun on Day 1 utilize Google Earth, creative interactive timeline software, research management programs (such as Zotero and RefWorks), document sharing (such as Google Docs and DropBox), and online research.

On Day 2, the film "Night and Fog" needs a projector or large monitor. Students may be given the option to use a personal computer or tablet for the "Holocaust Poetry" exercise, which requires access to an audio recording on YouTube.

Day 3's "The 'Auschwitz Selfie' Controversy" exercise uses a smartboard and document sharing (like Google Docs and DropBox). The "Painting the Holocaust" exercise utilizes internet research (either in class or as homework the previous evening), a smart board, and document sharing. Students may also be given the option to work with presentation software (such as PowerPoint) to create a mini-exhibition of Anselm Kiefer's works.

Day 4's "Kiefer and Celan" exercise needs a projector or large monitor for viewing artworks as a class. A projector or large monitor are also necessary for the "Oprah and Elie Wiesel at Auschwitz" activity, which has the students watching a video as a group.

Students may use personal computers or tablets to access the article read for the "'Night' as Art" activity on Day 5. The "Elie Wiesel Nobel Prize Acceptance Speech" activity requires a large monitor or projector for students to watch the video together as a group. Students may also use tablets or computers to draft their written responses to the prompts following the video.

Teacher Guide - Notes to the Teacher

Although every classroom is different, the immediacy of Wiesel's horrifying adolescent experience is likely to interest many students. The thought questions in this lesson plan provide material and ideas that students can use to write short original essays. For the sake of improving the power of expression, teachers should encourage students to write on topics that have been discussed in class, this time in the more formal writing style expected in a literary essay. At the same time, students should not be discouraged from choosing their own topics.

The questions provided for the final paper are most suitable for student essays. Remember that grading an essay should not depend on a simple checklist of required content.

The daily lessons can be expanded into additional days--or consolidated into fewer days--based on the needs of the students and the course.

Teacher Guide - Related Links

PBS -- "Elie Wiesel: First Person Singular"

http://www.pbs.org/eliewiesel/

Home page for 2002 PBS Video "Elie Wiesel: First Person Singular." Includes biographical and historical information, teaching guide, and other resources

PBS: Speak Truth to Power

http://www.pbs.org/speaktruthtopower/elie.html

Elie Wiesel biography and interview

PBS Video

http://video.pbs.org/search/?q=Elie+Wiesel

Several videos of Elie Wiesel

Elie Wiesel Nobel Prize Acceptance Speech

http://www.nobelprize.org/mediaplayer/index.php?id=2028

18-minute video of Elie Wiesel's Dec. 10, 1986 Nobel Prize acceptance speech

Oprah Winfrey Interviews Elie Wiesel

http://www.oprah.com/omagazine/Oprah-Interviews-Elie-Wiesel

Wiesel's interview with Oprah Winfrey.

The Elie Wiesel Foundation for Humanity

http://www.eliewieselfoundation.org/

The website for the foundation that Wiesel started with his wife Marion.

Academy of Achievement

http://www.achievement.org/autodoc/page/wie0int-1

Elie Wiesel interview

The New York Times Sunday Book Review: The Story of 'Night'

http://www.nytimes.com/2008/01/20/books/review/Donadio-t.html?pagewanted=all

The New York Review of Books: "An Open Letter to Elie Wiesel"

http://www.nybooks.com/articles/archives/1988/aug/18/an-open-letter-to-elie-wiesel/

The Guardian: Children's Books

http://www.theguardian.com/childrens-books-site/2014/aug/25/elie-wiesel-night-jewish-identity-amnesty-teen-takeover-2014

Book review of *Night*

United States Holocaust Memorial Museum

http://www.ushmm.org/

USHMM Holocaust Encyclopedia: Auschwitz

http://www.ushmm.org/wlc/en/article.php?ModuleId=10005189

USHMM Holocaust Encyclopedia entry for Auschwitz

USHMM Holocaust Encyclopedia: Elie Wiesel

http://www.ushmm.org/wlc/en/article.php?ModuleId=10007176

USHMM Holocaust Encyclopedia entry for Elie Wiesel

Auschwitz-Birkenau Memorial and Museum

http://en.auschwitz.org/m/

History Channel: Auschwitz

http://www.history.com/topics/world-war-ii/auschwitz

BBC Learning: School Radio

http://www.bbc.co.uk/schoolradio/subjects/history/ww2clips/children/fires

Audio clips from World War II, including radio news reports, speeches, songs and music, and "war sounds."

Old Radio World: World War II News Broadcasts

http://www.oldradioworld.com/shows/World_War_II_News_Broadcasts.php

Downloadable audio clips from World War II radio reports.

USHMM Online Exhibition: Nazi Propaganda

http://www.ushmm.org/propaganda/

United States Holocaust Memorial Museum interactive exhibition with timeline and image gallery of Nazi propaganda.

USHMM Mapping the Holocaust: Google Earth

http://www.ushmm.org/learn/mapping-initiatives/mapping-the-holocaust-google-earth

Instructions for downloading and using interactive Holocaust map with Google Earth.

USHMM Teaching About the Holocaust

http://www.ushmm.org/educators/teaching-about-the-holocaust

Educator resources for teaching about the Holocaust.

Teacher Guide - Night Bibliography

Lindsay Grant, author of Lesson Plan. Completed on January 19, 2015, copyright held by GradeSaver.

Updated and revised by Gemma Cooper-Novack January 30, 2015. Copyright held by GradeSaver.

Ruth Margalit. "Should Auschwitz Be a Site For Selfies?." The New Yorker. June 26, 2014. Jan. 11, 2015. <http://www.newyorker.com/culture/culture-desk/should-auschwitz-be-a-site-for-selfies>.

Chris Perez. "Smiling Auschwitz selfie sparks Twitter outrage." New York Post. July 21, 2014. Jan. 11, 2015. <http://nypost.com/2014/07/21/smiling-auschwitz-selfie-sparks-twitter-outrage/>.

Caitlin Dewey. "The other side of the infamous "Auschwitz selfie"." The Washington Post. July 22, 2014. Jan. 3, 2015. <http://www.washingtonpost.com/news/the-intersect/wp/2014/07/22/the-other-side-of-the-infamous-auschwitz-selfie/>.

Sue Hubbard. "Margarete (1981) by Anselm Kiefer (Saatchi collection)." The Independent. Oct. 24, 2008. Jan. 3, 2015. <http://www.independent.co.uk/arts-entertainment/art/great-works/margarete-1981-by-anselm-kiefer-saatchi-collection-970630.html>.

Rebecca Taylor. "Anselm Kiefer, Shulamite." Khan Academy. 2014. Jan. 3, 2015. <https://www.khanacademy.org/humanities/global-culture/identity-body/identity-body-europe/a/anselm-kiefer-shulamite>.

United States Holocaust Memorial Museum. "Elie Wiesel." USHMM Holocaust Encyclopedia . June 20, 2014. Jan. 3, 2015. <http://www.ushmm.org/wlc/en/article.php?ModuleId=10007176>.

Kerry Kennedy Cuomo. "Speak Truth to Power: Elie Wiesel." PBS. Jan. 3, 2015. <http://www.pbs.org/speaktruthtopower/elie.html>.

The Metropolitan Museum of Art. "Anselm Kiefer: Your Golden Hair, Margarete (2000.96.7)." Heilbrunn Timeline of Art History. October 2008. Jan. 3, 2015. <http://www.metmuseum.org/toah/works-of-art/2000.96.7>.

Ian Alteveer. "Anselm Kiefer (born 1945)." Heilbrunn Timeline of Art History. October 2008. Jan. 3, 2015. <http://www.metmuseum.org/toah/hd/kief/hd_kief.htm>.

Sarah Demuynck, Lucie Hladikova, Daniel Migdal, Aneta Tylawska, Geoffrey Walters, Norma Wright. "ACTS OF GENOCIDE COMMITTED SINCE THE ADOPTION OF THE CONVENTION ON THE PREVENTION AND PUNISHMENT OF THE CRIME OF GENOCIDE IN 1951." <u>Inter-Parliamentary Alliance for Human Rights and Global Peace</u>. Jan. 3, 2015. <<u>http://www.ipahp.org/index.php?en_acts-of-genocide</u>>.

Day 1 - Reading Assignment, Questions, Vocabulary

Read the first section of the novel, from the first line "They called him Moishe the Beadle..." to the point where Wiesel and his family are aboard the train transport, beginning "we were on our way." The first section is roughly 22 pages.

Common Core Objectives

- CCSS.ELA-LITERACY.W.9-10.2.A
  Introduce a topic; organize complex ideas, concepts, and information to make important connections and distinctions; include formatting (e.g., headings), graphics (e.g., figures, tables), and multimedia when useful to aiding comprehension.

- CCSS.ELA-LITERACY.W.9-10.2.B
  Develop the topic with well-chosen, relevant, and sufficient facts, extended definitions, concrete details, quotations, or other information and examples appropriate to the audience's knowledge of the topic.

- CCSS.ELA-LITERACY.RI.9-10.7
  Analyze various accounts of a subject told in different mediums (e.g., a person's life story in both print and multimedia), determining which details are emphasized in each account.

- CCSS.ELA-LITERACY.W.9-10.6
  Use technology, including the Internet, to produce, publish, and update individual or shared writing products, taking advantage of technology's capacity to link to other information and to display information flexibly and dynamically.

- CCSS.ELA-LITERACY.W.9-10.7
  Conduct short as well as more sustained research projects to answer a question (including a self-generated question) or solve a problem; narrow or broaden the inquiry when appropriate; synthesize multiple sources on the subject, demonstrating understanding of the subject under investigation.

- CCSS.ELA-LITERACY.W.9-10.8
  Gather relevant information from multiple authoritative print and digital sources, using advanced searches effectively; assess the usefulness of each

source in answering the research question; integrate information into the text selectively to maintain the flow of ideas, avoiding plagiarism and following a standard format for citation.

Note that it is perfectly fine to expand any day's work into two days depending on the characteristics of the class, particularly if the class will engage in all of the suggested classroom exercises and activities and discuss all of the thought questions.

Content Summary for Teachers

1

The book begins in Sighet, Transylvania in 1941. Elie Wiesel is thirteen years old. Extremely devout, Wiesel studies Kabbalah with a poor local man called Moishe the Beadle. The Hungarian police expel Moishe the Beadle, along with all the other foreign Jews, from Sighet. Months later, Moishe the Beadle returns to the town. He tells its residents about the horrors perpetrated by the Gestapo against the deportees. Nobody believes his tales of the mass killings. In the spring of 1944, Elie asks his father to buy the family emigration certificates to Palestine, but his father refuses. German Army soldiers arrive in Sighet, and are put up in Jewish homes. During Passover, the Germans arrest Jewish leaders. The Germans and Hungarian police enforce a series of laws affecting the Jewish community. First, Jews are required to stay in their homes for three days. Next, the Hungarian police seize all valuables from Jewish homes. Finally, all the Jews of Sighet are required to wear the yellow star of David. Two ghettos are established in the town. The Wiesel's home falls within the larger of the two ghettos. Elie's father reports that the ghettos will be evacuated and transports will begin. As the Jews of Sighet are systematically deported, those left remain optimistic. Elie's family is among the last to be deported. After twenty-four hours locked in the crowded synagogue, the Wiesels are loaded into a packed train car.

Thought Questions (students consider while they read)

1. Moishe the Beadle tells Elie "that every question possessed a power that was lost in the answer." What does Moishe the Beadle mean?

2. Why don't the people of Sighet listen to Moishe the Beadle? Why are his stories so easy to dismiss?

3. What was Elie like as a boy in Sighet? What does Wiesel emphasize about his younger self?

4. Why do the Jews of Sighet continue to deny evidence that they are facing a serious problem? Why do they carry on as normal until it is too late?

5. As the people of Sighet are systematically deported, their possessions--carefully packed, but ultimately abandoned--litter the streets. Of the abandoned houses, Wiesel writes: "It all belonged to everyone since it no longer belonged to anyone. It was there for the taking. An open tomb." What is the significance of these final lines of the passage? Why does Wiesel refer to the ghetto as "an open tomb"?

Vocabulary (in order of appearance)

"He was the jack-of-all-trades in a Hasidic house of prayer, a shtibl."

shtibl:

Yiddish: A small house of prayer for the Hasidic sect of the Jewish faith

"His waiflike shyness made people smile."

waiflike:

In the manner of a homeless or friendless person

"He sang, or rather he chanted, and the few snatches I caught here and there spoke of divine suffering, of the Shekhinah in Exile, where, according to Kabbalah, it awaits its redemption linked to that of man."

Shekhinah:

Hebrew: The dwelling of God's divine presence

Exile:

The location of one who has been barred from one's home country

A period in the sixth century BCE when the Jews were expelled from Jerusalem and forced to move to Babylon, the capital of the Chaldean empire in ancient Mesopotamia

Kabbalah:

An ancient, mystical tradition in Judaism

"By day I studied the Talmud and by night I would run to the synagogue to weep over the destruction of the Temple."

Talmud:

Ancient Jewish Rabbinical law, which is the textual basis of Orthodox Judaism

synagogue:

A Jewish house of worship

"You are too young for that, Maimonides tells us that one must be thirty before venturing into the world of mysticism, a world fraught with peril."

fraught:

Full of, loaded with

"He smiled indulgently."

indulgently:

Permissively, tolerantly

"He must not err and wish to enter the orchard through a gate other than his own."

err:

To make a mistake

"Not to learn it by heart but to discover with the very essence of divinity."

divinity:

Holiness, godliness

"A few days after they left, it was rumored that they were in Galicia, working, and even that they were content with their fate."

Galicia:

A medieval name for a region of Eastern Europe comprising modern-day Poland and western Ukraine

"The train with the deportees had crossed the Hungarian border and, once in Polish territory, had been taken over by the Gestapo."

Gestapo:

Secret police in Nazi-occupied Europe

"Some even insinuated that he only wanted their pity, that he was imagining things."

insinuated:

Suggested, implied

"London radio, which we listened to every evening, announced encouraging news: the daily bombings of Germany and Stalingrad, the preparation of the Second Front."

Stalingrad:

1942-43

City in the Soviet Union where major World War II battle, the 1952-53 "Battle of Stalingrad" was fought between German and Soviet armies

"My grandfather came to spend Rosh Hashanah with us so as to attend the services of the celebrated Rebbe of Borsche."

Rosh Hashana:

The Jewish New Year high holiday, celebrated for two days in early autumn

"And thus my elders concerned themselves with all manner of things--strategy, diplomacy, politics, and Zionism--but not with their own fate."

Zionism:

A nationalist, politial movement started in 1890 to establish a Jewish state in the Palestine region; this state would later become contemporary Israel

"I had asked my father to sell everything, to liquidate everything, and to leave."

liquidate:

To eliminate, get rid of something

"Budapest radio announced that the Fascist party had seized power."

Fascist:

A right-wing, authoritarian political govermental regime

In the mid-20th century, authoritarian political parties in Europe such as the National Socialist (Nazi) Party in Germany

"The regent Miklós Horthy was forced to ask a leader of the pro-Nazi Nyilas party to form a new government."

regent:

One who governs a region on behalf of the primary ruler

"Of course we had heard of the Fascists, but it was all in the abstract."

abstract:

Non-concrete, conceptual, theoretical

"The next day brought really disquieting news…"

disquieting:

Upsetting, unsettling

"Finally, people began to worry in earnest."

earnest:

Sincere, serious

Actively, genuinely

"The officers were billeted in private homes, even in Jewish homes."

billeted:

Temporarily stationed, lodged

"First edict: Jews were prohibited from leaving their residences for three days, under penalty of death."

edict:

Law, decree

"The same day, the Hungarian police burst into every Jewish home in town: a Jew was henceforth forbidden to own gold, jewelry, or any valuables."

henceforth:

From this point forward

"Then came the ghettos."

ghettos:

Areas in a city where specific ethnic or social groups are forced to live together, separate from the rest of the population

Zones designated for Jewish occupants

"A Jewish Council was appointed, as well as a Jewish police force, a welfare agency, a labor committee, a health agency--a whole governmental apparatus."

apparatus:

A multi-part mechanism in which all parts work together

"My father was running right and left, exhausted, consoling friends, checking with the Jewish Council just in case the order had been rescinded."

rescinded:

Taken back, reversed

"Valuable objects, precious rugs, silver candlesticks, Bibles and other ritual objects were strewn over the dusty grounds--pitiful relics that seemed never to have had a home."

relics:

Objects, often of religious significance, that are remnants of something otherwise lost

A pair of black cubes holding pieces of paper inscribed with Biblical verses and worn on the head and left arm of Jewish men, used to aid prayer

"Some of the Jewish police surreptitiously went to fill a few jugs."

surreptitiously :

Secretly, stealthily

"Slowly, heavily, the procession advanced toward the gate of the ghetto."

procession:

A group marching in a line or column from one destination to another

"His very presence in the procession was enough to make the scene seem surreal."

surreal:

Unreal, dreamlike

"It was like a page torn from a book, a historical novel, perhaps, dealing with the captivity in Babylon or the Spanish Inquisition."

Babylon :

An ancient Mesopotamian city in present-day Iraq, originally a Semitic administrative center in the Akkadian empire dating to the third century BCE

"The stars were but sparks of the immense conflagration that was consuming us."

conflagration:

A large, destructive fire

"They worry lest we join the partisans..."

partisans:

Members or supporters of a particular political party or cause

"There no longer was any distinction between rich and poor, notables and the others; we were all people condemned to the same fate--still unknown."

condemned:

Sentenced, fated

Additional Homework

1. Have students read the United States Holocaust Memorial Museum Holocaust Encyclopedia entry on Elie Wiesel.

2. Have students research Elie Wiesel. They should turn in the citation information for 4-5 articles, websites, or videos, with brief explanations of each source. For each source, they should also write a short paragraph or bullet-point list of what they learned.

3. Students should continue independent work on their long-term multimedia project.

Day 1 - Discussion of Thought Questions

1. Moishe the Beadle tells Elie "that every question possessed a power that was lost in the answer." What does Moishe the Beadle mean?

Time:

5 minutes

Discussion:

When asked why he prays, Elie responds that he doesn't know. His response is the essence of Moishe the Beadle's statement. God is mysterious, the universe is mysterious, man is mysterious--and it is through the process of seeking answers to difficult questions that one grows as an individual and builds a relationship with God. Moishe the Beadle suggests that no answer worth having is easily attained.

2. Why don't the people of Sighet listen to Moishe the Beadle? Why are his stories so easy to dismiss?

Time:

5 minutes

Discussion:

Students may consider the various motivations for ignoring Moishe the Beadle's warnings. He might be easy to dismiss because he is a kind of marginal figure in the community. The Jews of Sighet are fond of Moishe the Beadle, but he is poor and "had mastered the art of rendering himself insignificant, invisible." It may be because they are so accustomed to ignoring Moishe the Beadle that it is easy to brush off his warnings. He has great significance in Elie's life, but generally lacks authority in the community. Furthermore, his claims are unlike any the people of Sighet have yet heard, and they seem unbelievable. Students might also suggest that, as the cliché goes, people only hear what they want to. When he returns to Sighet after his escape from the Gestapo, Moishe the Beadle brings only damning information. It may have been easier for the community to remain optimistic and rely more on speculative reports of the war's imminent end, rather than Moishe the Beadle's tales of inhuman violence.

3. What was Elie like as a boy in Sighet? What does Wiesel emphasize about his younger self?

Time:

5 minutes

Discussion:

Wiesel portrays himself as a very curious, pious boy. Above all, he is focused on his religious studies. He is deeply curious, and seeks guidance in the unlikeliest of figures: Moishe the Beadle. Some students may compare the young Wiesel with themselves; to some, his religious devotion may seem foreign. They may observe that religion is the basis of the culture and community within which Wiesel is raised, and may compare and contrast this with their own lives.

4. Why do the Jews of Sighet continue to deny evidence that they are facing a serious problem? Why do they carry on as normal until it is too late?

Time:

5-10 minutes

Discussion:

The Jews of Sighet have their rights taken away gradually, over the course of several years. Students may observe that this incremental process makes each successive slight easier to bear. Even when they are forced to move into ghettos, the circumstances are bearable because families are kept together. When the German soldiers move into the village, they are mostly polite and unobtrusive. The people are as yet unaware of the unthinkable brutality of the camps. Students may suggest that it would have been impossible for the people of Sighet to imagine the unprecedented horrors awaiting them. If they had imagined "the worst," they still wouldn't have come close to the reality of the camps. Furthermore, by the time Elie and his family are deported from Sighet, the war is nearly over. It is more convenient for them to continue living as close to normal as possible, remaining optimistic that their circumstances are only temporary. Students may remark that it is generally difficult to break habits, and that choosing to leave Sighet without hard evidence supporting that decision would have seemed like too great a risk for many people. This may be an opportunity for students to discuss other examples of people denying clear evidence and waiting until it is too late to fix a problem, as in the contemporary case of global warming.

5. As the people of Sighet are systematically deported, their possessions--carefully packed, but ultimately abandoned--litter the streets. Of the abandoned houses, Wiesel writes: "It all belonged to everyone since it no longer belonged to anyone. It was there for the taking. An open tomb." What is the significance of these final lines of the passage? Why does Wiesel refer to the ghetto as "an open tomb"?

Time:

5 minutes

Discussion:

With this phrasing, Wiesel hints at the fate of his family and neighbors. When he arrives in the concentration camp, he sees bodies being burned in en masse. In this passage, Wiesel suggests that the residents of Sighet are, in a sense, already dead before they arrive in the camps. The moment they leave their homes and possessions behind, they resign themselves to imminent murder. The young Elie may have intuited this, but this line reads more like the author Wiesel retrospectively assessing the situation. Furthermore, students may discuss how one's home and belongings reflect one's life. They might discuss the topic of what a family's or an individual's belongings say about them--what stories objects tell. Without their residents and owners, these homes and objects are effectively "dead."

Day 1 - Short Answer Evaluation

1. Why do the residents of Sighet accept Moishe the Beadle, even though he is poor?

2. At the beginning of the novel, how does the young Wiesel spend his days and nights?

3. What reason does Elie's father give for refusing to find him a Kabbalah master?

4. What do Elie's parents do for a living?

5. With whom does Elie study Kabbalah?

6. Why does Elie cry when he prays?

7. Who are the first to be expelled from Sighet?

8. What was the punishment for breaking the edicts passed by the Germans and Hungarian police?

9. How do the Jews of Sighet react to being moved into ghettos?

_____

10. What do the police say will happen if anyone escapes from a train car?

_____

Answer Key

1. Moishe the Beadle has "mastered the art of rendering himself insignificant, invisible." He stays out of the way, and is charmingly clown-like.
2. During the day, he studies Talmud. At night, he goes to the synagogue to weep over the destruction of the Temple. Later, he spends his nights studying Kabbalah.
3. His father tells him he is too young, and that one must be thirty years old to begin exploring the mystical tradition.
4. They run a store.
5. Moishe the Beadle.
6. He doesn't know why he cries, only that he feels the need to do so.
7. The foreign Jews.
8. Breaking any edict was punishable by death.
9. They aren't afraid. They feel it is a good thing to be among their own people.
10. The person assigned to be in charge of that car will be shot.

Day 1 - Crossword Puzzle

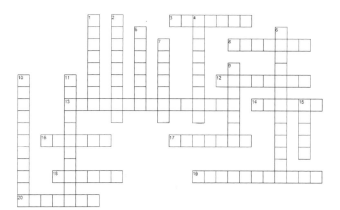

ACROSS

3. Authoritarian political regime
8. Youngest Wiesel sister
12. Ancient, mystical tradition in Judaism
13. secretly, stealthily
14. Transylvanian town where Wiesel grew up
16. Moishe the _____
17. Elie's street, in the first ghetto
18. Ancient Jewish Rabbinical law
19. Permissively, tolerantly
20. Secret police in Nazi Germany

DOWN

1. The eight days of _____
2. sentenced, fated
4. Jewish house of worship
5. full of, loaded with
6. Large, destructive fire
7. Saturday, the day of rest
9. ancient Mesopotamian city
10. upsetting, unsettling
11. Jewish New Year high holiday (two words)
15. law, decree

Crossword Puzzle Answer Key

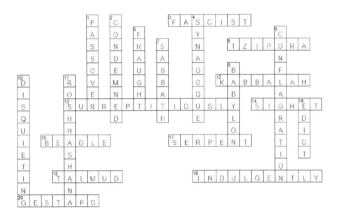

ACROSS

3. Authoritarian political regime
8. Youngest Wiesel sister
12. Ancient, mystical tradition in Judaism
13. secretly, stealthily
14. Transylvanian town where Wiesel grew up
16. Moishe the _____
17. Elie's street, in the first ghetto
18. Ancient Jewish Rabbinical law
19. Permissively, tolerantly
20. Secret police in Nazi Germany

DOWN

1. The eight days of _____
2. sentenced, fated
4. Jewish house of worship
5. full of, loaded with
6. Large, destructive fire
7. Saturday, the day of rest
9. ancient Mesopotamian city
10. upsetting, unsettling
11. Jewish New Year high holiday (two words)
15. law, decree

Day 1 - Vocabulary Quiz

Terms

1. _____ waiflike
2. _____ Kabbalah
3. _____ synagogue
4. _____ fraught
5. _____ indulgently
6. _____ Gestapo
7. _____ insinuated
8. _____ liquidate
9. _____ Fascist
10. _____ disquieting

Answers

A. Secret police in Nazi-occupied Europe
B. Authoritarian political regime
C. Upsetting, unsettling
D. To eliminate, get rid of something
E. In the manner of a homeless or friendless person
F. Suggested, implied
G. Full of, loaded with
H. A Jewish house of worship
I. permissively, tolerantly
J. An ancient, mystical tradition in Judaism

Answer Key

1. E waiflike: In the manner of a homeless or friendless person
2. J Kabbalah: An ancient, mystical tradition in Judaism
3. H synagogue: A Jewish house of worship
4. G fraught: Full of, loaded with
5. I indulgently: permissively, tolerantly
6. A Gestapo: Secret police in Nazi-occupied Europe
7. F insinuated: Suggested, implied
8. D liquidate: To eliminate, get rid of something
9. B Fascist: Authoritarian political regime
10. C disquieting: Upsetting, unsettling

Day 1 - Classroom Activities

1. Multimedia 'Night' Archive

Kind of Activity:

Long-term Project

Objective:

Students will be able to utilize technology and research in a multimedia presentation of the novel's sites, timeline, and major themes

Common Core Standards:

CCSS.ELA-LITERACY.W.9-10.6; CCSS.ELA-LITERACY.W.9-10.7; CCSS.ELA-LITERACY.W.9-10.8

Time:

40 minutes

Structure:

This long-term project is designed for students to connect the narrative in *Night* with corresponding historical events and broader historical themes, utilizing a wide range of media and technological tools. Students will create an interactive multimedia timeline and research archive based on the novel's events, geographies, and key figures. This project can be as structured or open-ended as you choose, depending upon student needs. Students will likely need more guidance in the early stages of the project, until they get a sense of the wealth of available resources they may mine for information to include in their archives.

There are numerous free interactive timeline programs available online, as well as those you can download for a fee. The interface you choose will determine the look and feel of each project, as well as the range of capabilities for linking images and files to particular dates and events. It may work best to have students work both in an interactive timeline and collect and organize files and links in a research management program, such as Zotero, RefWorks, or even a filesharing site like DropBox.

On this first day, have students explore the United States Holocaust Memorial Museum's Mapping the Holocaust: Google Earth project. Have them download Google Earth and the additional layers that will enable them to visualize particular sites referenced in the novel. Ask them to find Elie's home village of Sighet on a current map, and then to locate it on a map of Europe from 1942. What is different about these maps? What geographies have changed? This is the type of exercise that can, and should, lead to further research questions, and will serve as a model of activity for the duration of the project.

USHMM Mapping the Holocaust: Google Earth

http://www.ushmm.org/learn/mapping-initiatives/mapping-the-holocaust-google-earth

As the week progresses, students should investigate key figures mentioned (albeit briefly) in the novel, such as the notorious Dr. Mengele and Heinrich Himmler. Working individually or in pairs, students should conduct online research to find biographical information about these figures, as well as images and any pertinent video or audio recordings. You may need to guide students through the process of identifying useful, factual information from authoritative sources, and differentiating this from lay sources or spurious information. One objective of this project will be to train students to collect and organize their research information in a clear and logical manner.

As Elie's journey continues, have students look up information on the sites he describes in the novel: Sighet, Auschwitz, Birkenau, Buna, Gleiwitz, Buchenwald, etc. The USHMM Holocaust Encyclopedia is an incredibly rich resource, but community sites like Flickr and Tumblr can also be valuable sources.

Throughout the novel, Elie makes references to the war front. Students should include information about the progress of WWII in Europe in their timelines, connecting this with specific passages in the novel. For example, when Elie is in the infirmary and must choose whether to stay or be evacuated with the rest of the camp, what is happening militarily at that time? Where are the different troops located, and why is the camp evacuated?

For the last section of the novel, students should research the liberation of Buchenwald, connecting this event with the liberation of other concentration camps.

At the end of this project, students should have amassed a considerable bibliography and cache of relevant links, images, and files organized by topic.

Ideas for Differentiated Instruction:

This project can be adjusted to meet the needs of every student--it can be as structured or as open-ended as you choose. For students who need more support, you may wish to scaffold every step of the project, providing research terms and getting them started with resources. You may also wish to give them a step-by-step guide for organizing their research materials. Of course, you can also pair students who need more support with those who have stronger research, writing, and organizational skills to create a collaborative project. Some students may need additional support navigating online research and the various programs like Google Earth and the interactive timeline software. Be prepared to provide step-by-step instructions for using these interactive technological tools. Students with strong skills in these areas might be called upon to step into leadership roles, supporting their peers throughout the process.

Students who generally need a greater challenge can take real ownership over this project, both in its form and content. Students with special interests in particular areas--the arts, history, etc.--may be encouraged to do additional research on topics of their choice. Students with strong artistic skills may be encouraged to focus on their visual presentations.

For some students, the collection and organization of the material may be enough of a challenge, while you might encourage others to turn their research into a more focused multimedia resentation or a longer piece of writing.

Assessment Ideas:

Have students submit their timelines and archives for assessment. In addition to the number of sources collected for each topic, pay attention to the quality and variety of the selected sources.

If appropriate, and if time allows, you may also have students select one smaller topic from their overall archives and timelines to expand into a focused project. They may submit this project for further assessment, or present it to the class.

2. Understanding Genocide

Kind of Activity:

Long-term Project

Objective:

Students will be able to effectively research and present findings on other genocides around the world and throughout history

Common Core Standards:

CCSS.ELA-LITERACY.RI.9-10.7; CCSS.ELA-LITERACY.W.9-10.2.A; CCSS.ELA-LITERACY.W.9-10.2.B

Time:

45 minutes

Structure:

In American schools, the Holocaust is still the most commonly taught genocide; however, there have been several large-scale genocides around the world before and since the Holocaust. In this lesson, students will conduct research on other examples of genocide around the world. Working individually or in pairs, students will conduct extensive research on a particular case of genocide, and will organize and present their findings in a multimedia format. Each project should include written content, images, and any applicable audio-visual material. Students will not only ascertain the factual, historical information pertaining to their assigned 'case,' but--in the vein of their study of *Night*--will also research outspoken survivors, as well as important documentary and artistic responses, including memorials and museum exhibitions. Once completed, each project can be published to the class website, or uploaded to a document-sharing website like DropBox.

To get started, have students explore the following resources:

"Elie Wiesel: On the Atrocities in Sudan." These are remarks delivered at the Darfur Emergency Summit, convened at the Graduate Center of the City University of New York on July 14, 2004, by the American Jewish World Service and the United States Holocaust Memorial Museum. http://www.ushmm.org/wlc/en/article.php?ModuleId=10007205

The United States Holocaust Memorial Museum utilizes Google Earth to map the crisis in Darfur. Have students download the Google Earth layers and examine this crisis. http://www.ushmm.org/learn/mapping-initiatives/crisis-in-darfur

Investiage the Amnesty International website. http://www.amnestyusa.org/

As a class, discuss the definition of genocide. Did students know the word before this lesson? What did they think about genocide prior to this lesson? Did any of the sources they researched have differing definitions? Using an interactive whiteboard, record a list of known genocides around the world (provided by students). You may elect to have students choose their own case studies for in-depth research, or you may wish to assign individuals or pairs to a particular case. See the "Related Books" section for additional related readings, which may be a useful entrypoint for several case studies.

During the week, give students time for in-class reserach and writing, checking in on their progress.

Ideas for Differentiated Instruction:

For students who need more support, you can scaffold each step of this exercise. You may wish to pair them with another student who has strong research and writing skills. You might also want to provide them with a list of sources to get started, or a list of questions to guide their research.

Students who need a greater challenge can take real ownership over this exercise, which can be as structured or free-form as you choose. Consider suggesting an author or artist who has represented the particular act of genocide the student is researching. You might also assign additional reading material, or a documentary or feature film relating to their topic. For especially strong readers, consider assigning a memoir or historical text pertaining to their topic. Ask them to consider how this account compares with Wiesel's *Night*. Students with strong media skills can utilize a variety of technological tools for this project.

Assessment Ideas:

Have students submit their projects for assessment, either digitally or in hard copy. Consider the range and depth of research materials presented, and the level of interpretation and analysis applied to them. You might also assess the visual organization and presentation of these materials. You might also elect to have them present their project to the class, and assess the presentation.

Day 2 - Reading Assignment, Questions, Vocabulary

Read the section beginning with "Lying down was not an option..." and ending with "After four hours, we arrived at the new camp: Buna." This section is about 24 pages long.

Common Core Objectives

- CCSS.ELA-LITERACY.RL.9-10.7
  Analyze the representation of a subject or a key scene in two different artistic mediums, including what is emphasized or absent in each treatment (e.g., Auden's "Musée des Beaux Arts" and Breughel's Landscape with the Fall of Icarus).

- CCSS.ELA-LITERACY.RL.9-10.2
  Determine a theme or central idea of a text and analyze in detail its development over the course of the text, including how it emerges and is shaped and refined by specific details; provide an objective summary of the text.

Note that it is perfectly fine to expand any day's work into two days depending on the characteristics of the class, particularly if the class will engage in all of the suggested classroom exercises and activities and discuss all of the thought questions.

Content Summary for Teachers

2

At the start of this section, Wiesel, his parents and three sisters are traveling inside an overcrowded train car. Two days into the journey, the train stops in a Czechoslovakian border town. As they leave Hungary, the passengers are told they are now under the authority of the German Army. A fellow passenger, Mrs. Schächter, begins screaming about a fire. The others assume she has gone insane and is hallucinating due to thirst. After hours of her screaming, the other passengers turn on Mrs. Schächter and begin to beat her. The train arrives at Auschwitz. The passengers are optimistic upon hearing that conditions at the labor camp are good, and that families will be kept together. However, the SS immediately separate the men and women. Elie sees his mother and youngest sister for the last time. Elie considers killing himself when he learns that the SS is burning people--even small children and babies--at the camp. Elie and his father are assigned to their barrack.

They are stripped naked and sent to the barber to be shaved. Elie and his father are moved from Birkenau to Auschwitz, where they stay for three weeks. Elie is tattooed with the number A-7713. As unskilled laborers, Elie and his father are transferred to Buna.

Thought Questions (students consider while they read)

1. After attempting to placate her, the passengers in Elie's train car bind and gag Mrs. Schächter. How does Wiesel characterize this behavior? Based on his narrative, do you think this action was justified, or unnecessarily cruel?

2. After they bind and gag her, the deportees violently attack Mrs. Schächter in front of her young son. Why do you think they would be driven to such action?

3. Upon arriving at Auschwitz, Wiesel writes, "Nobody had ever heard that name." What connotations does the name Auschwitz have for you? Were you familiar with the camp prior to reading the novel? If so, what did you know about it?

4. How does Wiesel describe Auschwitz? Is there anything suprising about his characterization?

5. Elie feels remorse when he witnesses another inmate hit his father and does nothing. Why doesn't he react? Have you ever reacted to a situation in a way that surprised you, or made you feel like you didn't know yourself?

Vocabulary (in order of appearance)

"Our principle was to economize, to save for tomorrow. Tomorrow could be worse yet."

economize:

Minimize waste

To use sparingly, ration

"The doors were nailed, the way back irrevocably cut off."

irrevocably:

Permanently, irreversibly

"The world had become a hermetically sealed cattle car."

hermetically :

Airtight

"Her husband was a pious man who spent most of his days and nights in the house of study."

pious:

Observant of religious laws

"There was a tumult."

tumult:

Chaos, ruckus

"It was imperative to stay together."

imperative:

Absolutely necessary

"Another inmate appeared, unleashing a stream of invectives..."

invectives:

Harsh and contemptuous insults, accusations

"He looked like the typical SS officer: a cruel, though not unintelligent, face, complete with monocle."

monocle :

A single eyeglass, sometimes with a chain attached

"We did not know, as yet, which was the better side, right or left, which road led to prison and which to the crematoria."

crematoria :

Buildings used to burn bodies

"Mier Katz, a colossus, wore a child's pants, and Stern, a skinny little fellow, was floundering in a huge jacket."

colossus:

A gigantic statue, such as the ancient Greek bronze statue of Helios on the island of Rhodes

A giant man

"He harangued us from the center of the barrack..."

harangued :

Yelled at, verbally assaulted

"He looked at us as one would a pack of leprous dogs clinging to life."

leprous:

Showing signs of leprosy, an infectious disease of the nervous system causing skin lesions and disfiguration

Visibly diseased, ugly

"'Remember it always, let it be graven in your memories. ...'"

graven:

Permanently carved into, marked

"My father suddenly had a colic attack."

colic:

Abdominal, gastrointestinal pain

"The person looking for us was a small fellow with spectacles in a wizened face."

wizened :

Wrinkled, shriveled

Additional Homework

1. Have students read the USHMM Holocaust Encyclopedia entries for Auschwitz and Dr. Mengele.

2. To prepare for the following day's activity, have students read three articles about the "Auschwitz Selfie" controversy, about American teenager Breanna Mitchell, who posted a smiling photo of herself in the Auschwitz concentration camp to Twitter.

   The first article, "Smiling Auschwitz selfie sparks Twitter outrage," from the *New York Post*, briefly describes the online response to the photograph: http://nypost.com/2014/07/21/smiling-auschwitz-selfie-sparks-twitter-outrage/

   "The other side of the infamous 'Auschwitz selfie'" from the Washington Post delves deeper into the ordeal, including Mitchell's defense of her photo. The author considers the ethics of concentration camp selfies more broadly.

   http://www.washingtonpost.com/news/the-intersect/wp/2014/07/22/the-other-side-of-the-infamous-auschwitz-selfie/

A month prior to the "Auschwitz selfie" debacle, *The New Yorker* published an article titled "Should Auschwitz Be a Site for Selfies?"

Students should bring their annotated articles to class the following day, either in hard copy or on a personal tablet.

3. Have students read the entry for artist Anselm Kiefer on the Metropolitan Museum of Art's Heilbrunn Timeline of Art History: http://www.metmuseum.org/toah/hd/kief/hd_kief.htm

   Explore Kiefer's works on the Met Museum website, and do further research on his paintings. Each student should select three examples of Kiefer's paintings to discuss in class the following day. They should include the date, title, and medium of each selected work.

4. Students should continue independent work on their long-term multimedia and research projects.

Day 2 - Discussion of Thought Questions

1. After attempting to placate her, the passengers in Elie's train car bind and gag Mrs. Schächter. How does Wiesel characterize this behavior? Based on his narrative, do you think this action was justified, or unnecessarily cruel?

Time:

5 minutes

Discussion:

Students may consider in what circumstances the needs of the majority outweigh the fate of one individual. In this stressful and frightening situation, Mrs. Schächter's fear is contagious. Quieting her may help restore some modicum of peace for the rest of the passengers. Students may also pick up on the fact that the cruelty enacted upon the Jewish deportees by the Hungarian police and the Germans is similarly contagious--being forced to endure cramped conditions with little food and water, the deportees quickly begin to turn on one another. Students might discuss the limits of kindness between humans under duress.

2. After they bind and gag her, the deportees violently attack Mrs. Schächter in front of her young son. Why do you think they would be driven to such action?

Time:

5 minutes

Discussion:

As the story progresses, it becomes clear that violence is not only perpetrated against the Jewish prisoners by the SS; rather, there are several instances of violence between inmates. Dehumanization is a prominent theme throughout the book. In the camps, cruelty moves in all directions. The violence against Mrs. Schächter foreshadows future violence among inmates, and within the strange inmate power structures of the camp. Students may posit that Mrs. Schächter is something of a temporary scapegoat for the other passengers, who take their fear and exhaustion out on her. They translate their fear into anger, and direct it at a victim who has already been lost to grief. It might be suggested that anger is a more empowering and active emotion than fear.

3. Upon arriving at Auschwitz, Wiesel writes, "Nobody had ever heard that name." What connotations does the name Auschwitz have for you? Were you familiar with the camp prior to reading the novel? If so, what did you know about it?

Time:

5 minutes

Discussion:

This discussion will give you a good sense of students' prior knowledge of the novel's subject matter. You might use this opportunity to note students' ideas about Auschwitz, including any misconceptions, which you can bring back in later sections to gauge how understanding of the subject has changed. This may also be a time for students to share more personal connections with the Holocaust, or with Auschwitz more specifically.

4. How does Wiesel describe Auschwitz? Is there anything suprising about his characterization?

Time:

5 minutes

Discussion:

Wiesel's first impression of Auschwitz is that it's "better than Birkenau." He compares the cement barracks to Birkenau's wooden barracks, and notes the "little gardens here and there." Students may note how quickly Elie's perceptions adjust, given the relative basis of this assessment. Much like the gradual adjustment to increasingly difficult ways of life in Sighet, Elie is already searching for the positive in his horrific surroundings. It may also be surprising that there could be anything complementary to say about the notorious camp. Students may question why there would be such things as gardens decorating a factory of death.

5. Elie feels remorse when he witnesses another inmate hit his father and does nothing. Why doesn't he react? Have you ever reacted to a situation in a way that surprised you, or made you feel like you didn't know yourself?

Time:

5 minutes

Discussion:

This is one of the first instances where Elie's survival instinct trumps his loyalty to his father. He seems to instinctively know that he is better off not intervening in this situation, since any reaction would likely provoke further abuse; however, this instinct surprises him. He is beginning to see how the brutality of the camp tests even the strongest of familial bonds by placing individual survival above all else. This is an opportunity for students to relate their personal experiences to the novel. Some may empathize with Elie; others may disagree with his inaction.

Day 2 - Short Answer Evaluation

1. Why do the passengers in the train car physically assualt Mrs. Schächter?

    _____

2. Why do the passengers feel relief upon hearing Auschwitz is their final destination?

    _____

3. What happens to the personal belongings Elie and his fellow passengers brought with them on the train?

    _____

4. What does the angry inmate tell Elie and his father upon their arrival in Auschwitz?

    _____

5. What are the possible destinations for inmates after they appear before Dr. Mengele?

    _____

6. What does Elie see that prevents him from sleeping later in life?

    _____

7. By what means does Elie consider ending his own life?

    _____

8. What happens to the strongest-looking inmates?

    _____

9. What does Béla Katz write in the note he slips to Elie and his father?

_____

10. What phrase is written on the gates of Auschwitz, and what does it mean?

_____

Answer Key

1. Mrs. Schächter screams for hours about a fire nobody else can see.
2. They are told that conditions at the camp are good, and that families will be kept together. It is reported that the young will work in factories, while the elderly will work in the fields.
3. They are all left inside the train car when the passengers get to Birkenau.
4. He yells that they will be burned and turned into ashes.
5. Prison or the crematoria.
6. He sees small children and babies being burned in a ditch.
7. He considers running into the electrified fence.
8. The SS assign them to the Sonder-Kommando, the group that works in the crematoria.
9. That he was chosen for the Sonder-Kommando because of his strength, and was forced to burn his own father's body.
10. "Arbeit Macht Frei"--Work makes you free.

Day 2 - Crossword Puzzle

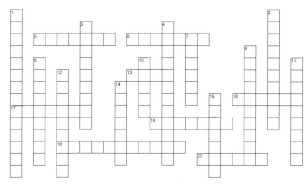

ACROSS

5. The notorious Dr. _____
6. wrinkled, shriveled
13. What Mrs. Schachter sees
16. permanently carved, marked
17. A single eyeglass
18. Prayer for the dead
19. permanently, irreversibly
20. Elie sees these being burned

DOWN

1. Those assigned to work in the crematoria (Two words)
2. harsh insults, accusations
3. At Birkenau, men and women get _____
4. airtight
7. Number of passengers in one train car
8. absolutely necessary
9. verbally assaulted
10. religiously observant
11. To use sparingly
12. The transport's "final destination"
14. Auschwitz gate says work means _____
15. Train stop on Czechoslovakian border

Crossword Puzzle Answer Key

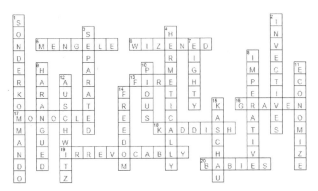

ACROSS

5. The notorious Dr. _____
6. wrinkled, shriveled
13. What Mrs. Schachter sees
16. permanently carved, marked
17. A single eyeglass
18. Prayer for the dead
19. permanently, irreversibly
20. Elie sees these being burned

DOWN

1. Those assigned to work in the crematoria (Two words)
2. harsh insults, accusations
3. At Birkenau, men and women get _____
4. airtight
7. Number of passengers in one train car
8. absolutely necessary
9. verbally assaulted
10. religiously observant
11. To use sparingly
12. The transport's "final destination"
14. Auschwitz gate says work means _____
15. Train stop on Czechoslovakian border

Day 2 - Vocabulary Quiz

Terms

1. _____ irrevocably
2. _____ pious
3. _____ imperative
4. _____ invectives
5. _____ monocle
6. _____ colossus
7. _____ harangued
8. _____ graven
9. _____ colic
10. _____ wizened

Answers

A. Wrinkled, shriveled
B. Observant of religious laws
C. Absolutely necessary
D. Harsh and contemptuous insults, accusations
E. A giant man
F. Permanently, irreversibly
G. Abdominal, gastrointestinal pain
H. Permanently carved into, marked
I. A single eyeglass
J. Yelled at, verbally assaulted

Answer Key

1. F irrevocably : Permanently, irreversibly
2. B pious: Observant of religious laws
3. C imperative: Absolutely necessary
4. D invectives: Harsh and contemptuous insults, accusations
5. I monocle: A single eyeglass
6. E colossus: A giant man
7. J harangued: Yelled at, verbally assaulted
8. H graven: Permanently carved into, marked
9. G colic: Abdominal, gastrointestinal pain
10. A wizened: Wrinkled, shriveled

Day 2 - Classroom Activities

1. Film: Night and Fog

Kind of Activity:

Classwide Discussion

Objective:

Students will be able to apply examples from documentary cinema to an analysis of the novel

Common Core Standards:

CCSS.ELA-LITERACY.RL.9-10.7

Time:

Time of film plus 20 minutes

Structure:

Together as a class, watch Alain Resnais' canonical 1955 documentary film *Night and Fog* (Criterion Collection). The film is approximately 32 minutes long, in French with English subtitles. Resnais uses archival photographs and his own cinematography to starkly narrate the horrors of Auschwitz. You may wish to alert students that the film contains some disturbing imagery and brief nudity (in a photograph of camp inmates.)

After the film, allow ten to fifteen minutes of free writing time for students to record their reactions, impressions, and questions.

In small groups of 4-5 or together as a class, discuss the following:

1. What is the purpose of Resnais' alternating use of black-and-white still images and color moving images? What effect do these transitions have?

The movement between color and black-and-white, motion and still imagery, signals a chronological shift in the film. The color cinematography places the viewer in Resnais' contemporary moment, years after Aushwitz has closed. The black-and-white images take the viewer backwards in time, documenting life during the camp's operation and liberation. Students should consider Resnais' manipulation of the medium to tell a story.

2. Resnais narrates: "The masses, taken by surprise, by error, or by chance begin their journey to the camps." Did Wiesel's family get transported to the camps by surprise, error, or chance? How would you characterize their particular tragedy? Point to specific passages in the text to support your claims.

3. In the second half of the film, Resnais posits "What hope do we have, of truly capturing this reality?" What challenges does the author or artist face in attempting to represent the Holocaust? Why is this subject so difficult to articulate? Would you say that *Night*, as a written narrative, is more or less powerful as an informational source about the Holocaust than *Night and Fog*? How about as a work of art?

4. Discuss the prominence of "Night" in the titles of both works. What significance does this word have in each work? What does it symbolize?

Ideas for Differentiated Instruction:

For students who need extra support, consider providing focused questions prior to the film, or a sheet for scaffolding notes during the film.

If equal participation is a concern, consider having students work in small discussion groups. Pair more outspoken students with quieter students, and check in with groups to ensure all voices are heard.

Assessment Ideas:

Have students write a summary of *Night and Fog*, including descriptions of its formal and narrative qualities. What did they learn from the film? Did it change their experience of reading the novel? Why or why not?

2. Holocaust Poetry: Paul Celan's "Death Fugue"

Kind of Activity:

Classwide Discussion

Objective:

Students will be able to evaluate representation of the Holocaust in another literary medium and compare with themes of the novel

Common Core Standards:

CCSS.ELA-LITERACY.RL.9-10.2

Time:

40 minutes

Structure:

Poet and translator Paul Celan (1920-1970) was born Paul Antschel to German-speaking Jewish parents in present-day Ukraine, then the Kingdom of Romania. During World War II, Celan worked in a forced labor camp for 18 months; his parents were killed in a concentration camp. After the war, Celan lived in Bucharest, Vienna, and Paris. He committed suicide in 1970. The author of several books of poetry, Celan is perhaps best known for his poem "Death Fugue" (*Tödesfuge* in German), which evokes the horrors of the Nazi concentration camps.

In this lesson, students will consider how Celan manipulates language in poetic form to address the atrocities of the Holocaust. They will compare Wiesel's narrative form with Celan's metaphoric and symbolic language.

Begin the lesson with a brief introduction to Celan's biography, but do not tell them anything specific about the poem they will read. Part of the goal of the exercise is to encourage students to arrive at the poem's subject matter through close reading and analysis. Its themes will likely become clear in the discussion, especially given the context of Celan's biography; however, you may need to guide students toward this understanding. Provide each student with a copy of the poem, or have them access the poem on a personal tablet or computer. Have students read the poem silently to themselves, underlining unfamiliar words and noting significant lines and passages. Have a volunteer read the poem aloud, or have students trade off reading each line; the purpose is to hear the words spoken aloud. Students may continue annotating the poem.

First, ask students to share what they notice about the poem. This can be any observation, and does not have to be "significant"--they should simply note something they see or hear in the poem that they can point to concretely (the "noticing" should be observable by all.) You might spend as long as ten minutes on this "noticing" stage--it may feel somewhat tedious, but will encourage close reading and draw out aspects of the text that may not have been noticed by all.

Next, ask students what they think is going on in the poem. Have them point to specific lines or passages of the text to support their inferences. What questions do they have about the text? What is confusing or unclear? By this point, students may have already identified the subject of the poem, but may need further guidance. Ask them to consider why Celan has chosen to represent the death camps in this form. What is the poem's tone? What imagery does the poem conjure? How does Celan's language--from word choice to structure and cadence--evoke the horrors of the camps?

Listen to a recording of Celan reciting "Death Fugue" in its original language, German. You can access a recording at the following link: https://www.youtube.com/watch?v=pHgYRtefUqs. Ask students to pay special attention to Celan's tone and pacing. What kind of mood does his voice convey as he reads? Is it possible to glean the poem's meaning without understanding every (or any) of the words?

Finally, ask students to discuss how Celan's artistic response to the Holocaust compares with what they've read of *Night*. What are the advantages/disadvantages of representing this difficult subject in a poetic versus a narrative form. What is successful or unsuccessful about each author's literary depiction of the Holocaust?

Ideas for Differentiated Instruction:

When reading the poem aloud, you might encourage strong readers or performers to recite the poem for the class. Otherwise, you might encourage more reserved or less confident students to take on the role, or split the poem by line or section to include multiple orators.

To encourage equal participation, consider having every student share aloud one thing they notice in the poem.

Assessment Ideas:

Consider having students write a short essay response comparing *Night* and "Death Fugue," focusing on how each author uses language to convey a shared subject.

Day 3 - Reading Assignment, Questions, Vocabulary

Read the section beginning with "The camp looked as though it had been through an epidemic: empty and dead" and ending with "That night, the soup tasted of corpses." This section is about 18 pages long.

Common Core Objectives

- CCSS.ELA-LITERACY.SL.9-10.1.A
  Come to discussions prepared, having read and researched material under study; explicitly draw on that preparation by referring to evidence from texts and other research on the topic or issue to stimulate a thoughtful, well-reasoned exchange of ideas.

- CCSS.ELA-LITERACY.SL.9-10.1.B
  Work with peers to set rules for collegial discussions and decision-making (e.g., informal consensus, taking votes on key issues, presentation of alternate views), clear goals and deadlines, and individual roles as needed.

Note that it is perfectly fine to expand any day's work into two days depending on the characteristics of the class, particularly if the class will engage in all of the suggested classroom exercises and activities and discuss all of the thought questions.

Content Summary for Teachers

3

At Buna, the inmates have a medical and dental inspection. The dentist keeps track of those who have gold teeth. The reader is introduced to a Polish Jew named Juliek, who plays violin in the camp orchestra. (Juliek returns in an important scene in the final section of the novel.) Elie is assigned to a Kommando and must work in an electrical factory. Elie is sent to the dentist to have his gold crown removed, but is able to convince the dentist to postpone the extraction. He eventually has the crown removed when a Pole named Franek threatens him. Elie and his father are bullied by a Kapo named Idek. A kind Frenchwoman, a forced labor inmate also working in the factory, comforts Elie after Idek beats him. Years later, Elie sees her on a train in Paris and finds out she concealed her Jewish identity in the camps. Idek has Elie whipped after Elie interrupts him having sex with a young girl. An inmate is shot for eating soup from an unattended cauldron. An American air strike on Buna destroys several buildings. Elie witnesses several hangings. He is particularly affected by the hanging of one kind child assistant to an *Oberkapo*.

Thought Questions (students consider while they read)

1. What is the significance of Wiesel's reminiscence of his encounter with the kind French woman from Buna on the Paris métro years after the war? What does this digression add to the story?

2. How does Wiesel describe the extreme hunger he experienced in the camps? What were the psychological impacts of his starvation?

3. What effect do the public executions have on Elie's morale? Why do you think the SS would stage public hangings, when the guards so often unceremoniously shoot prisoners?

4. Discuss the final line of the chapter: "That night, the soup tasted of corpses." What is the significance of this line in the context of the preceding passages?

5. How does Wiesel describe the Germans and other authority figures in the camp? What kind of images do these descriptions conjure?

Vocabulary (in order of appearance)

"...there existed a veritable traffic of children among homosexuals, I learned later."

veritable:

True, utter

"...there existed a veritable traffic of children among homosexuals, I learned later.)"

traffic:

The transportation of people, goods, or vehicles along a particular route

Illicit or illegal exchange or sale of people

"'...For a pittance: your shoes. ...'"

pittance:

A very small amount

"And so we would sometimes hum melodies evoking the gentle waters of the Jordan River and the majestic sanctity of Jerusalem."

sanctity:

Holiness, sacredness

"We decided that if we were allowed to live until the Liberation, we would not stay another day in Europe. We would board the first ship to Haifa."

Haifa:

A port city in the Levant, in Palestine at the time of the events in the book

"Seated in the chair, I asked meekly: 'What are you going to do, sir?'"

meekly:

Timidly, shyly

"'You old loafer!' he started yelling."

loafer:

A lazy person, a layabout

"It was untenable."

untenable :

Unsustainable, unmanagable

"I had a novel experience."

novel:

New

"He moved one hundred prisoners so that he could copulate with this girl!"

copulate:

Have sexual intercourse

"The last sound of the American plane dissipated in the wind and there we were, in our cemetery."

dissipated:

Scattered, disintegrated

Decreasing, eventually disappearing

"One week later, as we returned from work, there, in the middle of the camp, in the Appelplatz, stood a black gallows."

gallows:

Wooden structure used for executions by hanging

"His manacled hands did not tremble."

manacled:

Shackled, handcuffed

"The SS seemed more preoccupied, more worried, than usual."

preoccupied:

Distracted, absorbed in thought

Additional Homework

1. Students should continue independent work on their long-term multimedia and research projects.

Day 3 - Discussion of Thought Questions

1. What is the significance of Wiesel's reminiscence of his encounter with the kind French woman from Buna on the Paris métro years after the war? What does this digression add to the story?

Time:

5 minutes

Discussion:

The bit of hope the woman gave him in a vulnerable moment was significant and memorable for Elie. As he learns from speaking with her later, both of them were simply doing their best to survive the camps. The personal risk the woman assumed in extending a small kindness to Elie serves to counterbalance the random cruelty of Idek's assault on Elie.

2. How does Wiesel describe the extreme hunger he experienced in the camps? What were the psychological impacts of his starvation?

Time:

5 minutes

Discussion:

Elie's extreme hunger removes the nuance from his emotional life. He becomes singularly focused on and motivated by his hunger and the pursuit of food. This starvation is part of the systematic dehumanization of the camps, as prisoners are forced to scavenge like animals to survive.

3. What effect do the public executions have on Elie's morale? Why do you think the SS would stage public hangings, when the guards so often unceremoniously shoot prisoners?

Time:

5 minutes

Discussion:

Elie is unfazed by the public executions, with the exception of the young *pipel*. It is clear that the prisoners become increasingly desensitized to the constant murder around them. His perpetual state of starvation distracts Elie from feeling emotions like pity or sorrow for too long, or at all. Students may remark about the transformative power of hunger. They may also speculate that the SS stages these public executions precisely to diminish the prisoners' morale. Historically, this type of execution was meant to be instructive to the masses--a threat of what would happen if one defied authority. The prisoners hanged at the camp gallows are used as examples for the other inmates, who are made to live in unending fear of death.

4. Discuss the final line of the chapter: "That night, the soup tasted of corpses." What is the significance of this line in the context of the preceding passages?

Time:

5 minutes

Discussion:

Previously, after watching public hangings in the camp, Elie writes that the soup tasted "better than ever." This line underscores the all-consuming power of hunger, which minimizes even the horrific scene of public execution. After Elie witnesses the hanging of the beloved *pipel,* who suffers a prolonged death, he cannot even enjoy his soup. That the *pipel*'s suffering outweighs Elie's hunger, tainting the taste of the soup, emphasizes the extreme emotional effect of the event. This is a rare moment when Elie is reminded of his own humanity in the dehumanizing world of the camp.

5. How does Wiesel describe the Germans and other authority figures in the camp? What kind of images do these descriptions conjure?

Time:

5 minutes

Discussion:

Wiesel's descriptive language helps to characterize these figures as villians. The tent leader with "an assassin's face, fleshy lips, and hands like a wolf's paws." Mengele's "cruel, but not unintelligent" face. They drive home the separation between the prisoners and the powerful.

Day 3 - Short Answer Evaluation

1. What does the tent leader's aide want in exchange for getting Elie to a good Kommando?

_____

2. What is the camp dentist looking for?

_____

3. Why can't Juliek the violinist play Beethoven?

_____

4. What do Elie and his friends Yossi and Tibi decide they will do if they survive until the Liberation?

_____

5. How does Elie avoid having his gold crown removed?

_____

6. Why is the Czechoslovakian Jewish dentist imprisoned and sentenced to hanging?

_____

7. What does the kind Frenchwoman reveal to Elie when he sees her in Paris after the war?

_____

8. Who was the "only victim" of the American air strike on Buna?

_____

9. How is the Dutchman's young servant different from the other 'pipels'?

_____

10. Why doesn't the Dutchman's 'pipel' die immediately when he is hanged from the gallows?

_____

Answer Key

1. He wants Elie's shoes.
2. Gold teeth.
3. Jews are not allowed to play German music.
4. They will leave Europe immediately for Haifa.
5. He tells the dentist he is sick and has a fever.
6. He has been selling the prisoners' gold teeth for personal profit.
7. That she is Jewish, and had hidden the fact that she spoke German.
8. The man who was shot by the SS for eating from a cauldron of soup.
9. He is kind, whereas the other pipels are especially cruel.
10. He is just a child, and is too light.

Day 3 - Crossword Puzzle

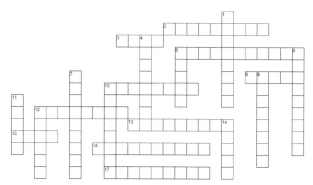

ACROSS

2. unsustainable
3. Person in charge of a Kommando
5. absorbed in thought
8. Israeli port city
10. shackled
12. The orchestra plays a _____ march
13. Composer; Jews are forbidden to play his music
15. Kapo who beats Elie's father
16. scattered, disintegrated
17. The camp dentist looks for these (Two words)

DOWN

1. holiness, sacredness
4. A very small amount
5. Young assistant to the Oberkapo
6. Dentist has a face like a _____ _____ (Two words)
7. True, utter
9. An _____ plane bombs the Buna factory
10. Elie helps his father practice this
11. City where Elie sees kind Frenchwoman after the war
12. timidly, shyly
14. new

Crossword Puzzle Answer Key

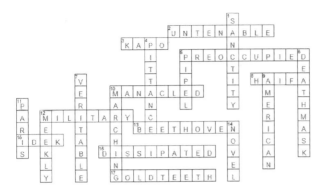

ACROSS

2. unsustainable
3. Person in charge of a Kommando
5. absorbed in thought
8. Israeli port city
10. shackled
12. The orchestra plays a _____ march
13. Composer; Jews are forbidden to play his music
15. Kapo who beats Elie's father
16. scattered, disintegrated
17. The camp dentist looks for these (Two words)

DOWN

1. holiness, sacredness
4. A very small amount
5. Young assistant to the Oberkapo
6. Dentist has a face like a _____ _____ (Two words)
7. True, utter
9. An _____ plane bombs the Buna factory
10. Elie helps his father practice this
11. City where Elie sees kind Frenchwoman after the war
12. timidly, shyly
14. new

Day 3 - Vocabulary Quiz

Terms

1. _____ veritable
2. _____ pittance
3. _____ sanctity
4. _____ copulate
5. _____ meekly
6. _____ untenable
7. _____ novel
8. _____ dissipated
9. _____ manacled
10. _____ preoccupied

Answers

A. Have sexual intercourse
B. Scattered, disintegrated
C. Holiness, sacredness
D. True, utter
E. Unsustainable, unmanageable
F. Timidly, shyly
G. Shackled, handcuffed
H. New
I. Distracted, absorbed in thought
J. A small amount

Answer Key

1. D veritable: True, utter
2. J pittance: A small amount
3. C sanctity: Holiness, sacredness
4. A copulate: Have sexual intercourse
5. F meekly: Timidly, shyly
6. E untenable : Unsustainable, unmanageable
7. H novel: New
8. B dissipated: Scattered, disintegrated
9. G manacled: Shackled, handcuffed
10. I preoccupied: Distracted, absorbed in thought

Day 3 - Classroom Activities

1. The 'Auschwitz Selfie' Controversy

Kind of Activity:

Group Discussion

Objective:

Students will be able to form a reasoned opinion on the contemporary ethics of photographing in concentration camps

Common Core Standards:

CCSS.ELA-LITERACY.SL.9-10.1.A

Time:

40 minutes

Structure:

In *Night and Fog*, Alain Resnais says, "A crematorium from the outside can look like a picture postcard. Today tourists have their snapshots taken in front of them." Resnais's narration indicates that the practice of taking personal photographs at the sites of former concentration camps has been occurring at least since 1955, the year of the film's release. This lesson asks students to consider the ethics of taking photos at concentration camps by analyzing a contemporary controversy on the subject. In 2014, an American teenager named Breanna Mitchell made the news when she posted a smiling 'selfie' in the Auschwitz concentration camp to Twitter, along with a smiling emoji. Students should come to class prepared to discuss this event, having read and reflected upon three relevant articles assigned as homework the previous day.

You might begin the discussion as a whole class by asking students if they take selfies. When and why do they take pictures of themselves, and where do they post them? What kinds of responses to their selfies do they hope for or expect?

In small groups of 4-6, ask students to discuss the following questions:

1. How did Mitchell justify her choice to take and post this photo?

2. Why did she experience such backlash for the photo?

3. Do you think Mitchell was right in posting this photo? Why or why not?

4. Is it ever appropriate to take happy or silly photographs at a concentration camp? Why or why not?

As a whole class, ask each group to share its answers to questions three and four. Using an interactive whiteboard, create a two-column list with one column for "pro-selfie" and one for "anti-selfie." Record the arguments for both. Upload these to the class website or share them using a filesharing website such as Dropbox or GoogleDocs.

Ideas for Differentiated Instruction:

Consider asking students with strong writing and organizational skills to act as group stenographers, recording the group's discussion of each question as it unfolds.

For students who need extra support, consider providing guiding questions or a sheet scaffolding notetaking for the preliminary parts of this lesson.

You may also consider inviting less outspoken students (or, alternately, students with strong presentation skills) to speak on behalf of the group during the whole-class portion of the lesson.

Assessment Ideas:

1. Have each student submit a written response (digital or hard copy) to the first two prompts for group discussion, citing information from the assigned articles.

2. Have students write a short essay defending either a pro- or anti-selfie stance based on the Mitchell controversy. Essays should cite information from the assigned research. You may also ask students to incorporate one to two additional sources based on additional research on the topic.

2. Painting the Holocaust: Anselm Kiefer

Kind of Activity:

Group Work

Objective:

Students will be able to describe and analyze visual representations of Holocaust subject matter

Common Core Standards:

CCSS.ELA-LITERACY.SL.9-10.1.B

Time:

1 hour

Structure:

Contemporary artist Anselm Kiefer, born in 1945 and raised in a divided postwar Germany, takes on his country's fraught history in his mixed-media paintings. Kiefer's work, which often engages the Holocaust, is part of the permanent collections of many prominent art museums across the globe. This lesson will introduce students to Kiefer's work, and help them build skills in visual description and analysis. Ultimately, students will be able to evaluate Kiefer's visual strategies for representing the Holocaust, and compare his methods to Wiesel's literary account. In 2014, the Massachusetts Museum of Contemporary Art (MASS MoCA) installed a long-term solo exhibition of Kiefer's work, which will be in the museum's galleries until 2028. The museum describes Kiefer's work as follows: "The artist often builds his imagery on top of photographs, layering his massive canvases with dirt, lead, straw, and other materials that generate a 'ground' that reads literally of the earth itself. Within these thick, impastoed surfaces Kiefer embeds textual or symbolic references to historic figures or places: these become encoded signals through which Kiefer invokes and processes history."

Students should come to this lesson with three images of Kiefer's work, having read a short biography of the artist on the Metropolitan Museum of Art's Heilbrunn Timeline of Art History as homework the night before. (If you choose not to assign this as homework prior to the lesson, allow 25-30 minutes of in-class internet research time prior to the lesson. It is important that students come to the discussion with some background knowledge of Kiefer, and with three printed images of his work.) Starting in small groups of 3-4, students will share their chosen works and explain why they have selected each. After each student has shared his or her selected works, the group should arrange the images in chronological order. If applicable, you might encourage each group to think about how the subject, materials, or techniques of the works appear to change over time. You might also guide students to consider whether and how Kiefer's works are literal or symbolic, how his materials and titles relate (or don't) to the subject matter, and how Kiefer's biography might have informed these choices. After arranging the works according to date, the students should collaboratively generate a list of approximately 5-10 descriptive terms that apply to all of the images in the assembled mini-collection. Ask students to imagine they are curators planning an exhibit of all the works they have individually selected. Together, each group should write 2-3 sentences describing Kiefer's work. These sentences should connect the descriptive terms with Kiefer's biography.

As an entire class, have each group report its list of terms. Using a smartboard, record these terms. Make sure to note which terms, if any, are repeated by multiple groups. Upload this file to the course website, and/or make it accessible to all students via a document sharing website such as DropBox or Google Docs.

Finally, have each group "mount" its mini-exhibition. You may choose to have students produce their exhibits digitally, posting their "curatorial statements" and all selected images to the course website. This can also be done in a PowerPoint presentation, to be shared with the rest of the class. You might also choose to have them write out their "curatorial statements" on construction paper and tack these up, along with all of the group's printed images, around the classroom. If you choose the latter option, allow time for each group to walk around and look at the other mini-exhibits.

Once every group has had the opportunity to review every other group's work, reconvene as a whole class. Discuss Kiefer's stategies for representing the Holocaust visually. How is Kiefer's highly symbolic, semi-abstract style effective (or not) in representing this difficult subject matter? How is this kind of representation different from the documentary imagery the students have seen in Alain Resnais's *Night and Fog*? Are there any similarities between Kiefer's work and Wiesel's written narrative? Do the two utilize any of the same symbolic language?

Ideas for Differentiated Instruction:

Ideally, the small groups will be as diverse as possible in terms of student skill level and interests. This structure provides a good opportunity for students with strong leadership and organizational skills to help guide discussion and keep the group on task; alternately, you may wish to give less outspoken students the chance to act as group leader. You may wish to structure the time of each part of this lesson somewhat rigidly, and might assign one student in each group to keep the others on track. When the small groups first come together, you may consider giving each student the same amount of time (roughly 2-3 minutes) to share his or her selected works and explain the reasons for these choices.

In the initial research and image selection process, consider pairing students who need more support with students who have demonstrated strong research, reading, and artistic skills. If students are working in pairs, they should choose six images to present to the small groups instead of three.

If you feel the class as a whole needs more support in working with contemporary art, consider providing each group with examples of descriptive terminology. You might also provide them with examples of curatorial text about Kiefer to give them a better understanding of the kind of language used in this context. There are many great examples of writing on Kiefer available on the websites of major art museums like MASS MoCA.

For students who need an extra challenge, ask them to think about what other ways-- besides chronologically--the group's images might be organized (thematically, by material components, etc.)

Assessment Ideas:

1. Have each group submit its digital mini-exhibition and curatorial statement for assessment, noting which student originally selected which images.

2. Ask students to write a short reflection on the process of putting together their images and coming up with a concise descriptive statement. What was challenging about this process? Was their any disagreement between group members? How were these differences reconciled?

3. Have students submit a detailed written description of one of Kiefer's works.

Day 4 - Reading Assignment, Questions, Vocabulary

Read the section beginning with "The summer was coming to an end" and ending with "It snowed on and on." This section is about 18 pages long.

Common Core Objectives

- CCSS.ELA-LITERACY.SL.9-10.1.C
  Propel conversations by posing and responding to questions that relate the current discussion to broader themes or larger ideas; actively incorporate others into the discussion; and clarify, verify, or challenge ideas and conclusions.

- CCSS.ELA-LITERACY.RL.9-10.4
  Determine the meaning of words and phrases as they are used in the text, including figurative and connotative meanings; analyze the cumulative impact of specific word choices on meaning and tone (e.g., how the language evokes a sense of time and place; how it sets a formal or informal tone).

- CCSS.ELA-LITERACY.RL.9-10.9
  Analyze how an author draws on and transforms source material in a specific work (e.g., how Shakespeare treats a theme or topic from Ovid or the Bible or how a later author draws on a play by Shakespeare).

Note that it is perfectly fine to expand any day's work into two days depending on the characteristics of the class, particularly if the class will engage in all of the suggested classroom exercises and activities and discuss all of the thought questions.

Content Summary for Teachers

4

On Rosh Hashana, Elie has a crisis of faith. On Yom Kippur, he refuses to fast. Elie is transferred to the construction Kommando, where he does hard labor. He encounters Dr. Mengele during another inspection. For a time it seems Elie's father may be chosen for selection, but he is miraculously spared. Winter comes, and Elie must have an operation on his swollen foot. The Russians approach as Elie recovers in the infirmary. He must choose whether to be evacuated with the rest of the camp, or risk staying in the infirmary. Just two days after his surgery, Elie returns to his block to be evacuated with the others. The SS lead the inmates on a harrowing march through the snowy night.

Thought Questions (students consider while they read)

1. Why do you think the inmates are compelled to gather for prayer on the eve of Rosh Hashana? What effect does this gathering have on Elie?

2. What does the anecdote about Akiba Drumer suggest about Elie's own faith in God?

3. Why does another patient in the infirmary tell Elie he has "more faith in Hitler than in anyone else"? What does he mean when he says "He alone has kept his promises, all his promises, to the Jewish people"?

4. If you were in Elie's position, would you have chosen to stay in the infirmary, or left camp with the rest of the evacuees?

5. Why is it ironic that the *Blockälteste* makes the inmates clean the bunks one hour before the camp's evacuation?

Vocabulary (in order of appearance)

"How do You compare to this stricken mass gathered to affirm to You their faith, their anger, their defiance?"

stricken:

Characterized by grief or misfortune

"What does Your grandeur mean, Master of the Universe, in the face of all this cowardice, this decay, and this misery?"

grandeur :

Greatness, impressiveness

Great holiness

"Some ten thousand men had come to participate in a solemn service, including the Blockälteste, the Kapos, all bureaucrats in the service of Death."

bureaucrats:

An official, as in a government or business, who adheres to policy and routine

"Thousands of lips repeated the benediction, bent over like trees in a storm."

benediction:

Words of blessing or affirmation

Religious blessing

"I was not longer able to lament."

lament:

To feel or express sadness, mourning, or regret

"Yom Kippur. The Day of Atonement."

atonement:

The forgiveness of wrongful deeds or sins; reconciliation

"That evening he announced to us that henceforth no one was allowed to leave the block after the evening soup."

henceforth:

From this point forward

"Three SS officers surrounded the notorious Dr. Mengele, the very same who had received us in Birkenau."

notorious:

Widely known for a bad reason; infamous

"A poor emaciated Jew questioned him anxiously, his voice trembling ..."

emaciated:

Unnaturally thin

Excessively thin and sickly due to starvation

"My father had a present for me: a half ration of bread, bartered for something he had found at the depot, a piece of rubber that could be used to repair a shoe."

bartered:

Negotiated a trade, haggled

"All that mattered was to be far from the block, far form the crucible of death, from the center of hell."

crucible :

A container or furnace used in metallurgy, heated to high temperatures

A severe test or trial

"All day, I plodded around like a sleepwalker."

plodded:

Walked slowly and with great effort

"But as soon as he felt the first chinks in his faith, he lost all incentive to fight and opened the door to death."

chinks:

A small hole or opening, as in defensive armor

incentive:

Motivation, sense of purpose

"The veterans grabbed the opportunity for further sniggering"

sniggering:

Snickering, cruel laughter

"The doctor, a great Jewish doctor, a prisoner like ourselves, was categorical..."

categorical:

Unconditional, absolute

"I barely understood what he was telling me, but the inflection of his voice soothed me."

inflection:

A particular change in tone of voice

"The death knell."

knell:

A mournful sign or sound, as in the ringing of a bell at a funeral.

Additional Homework

1. Students should continue working on original Kiefer-inspired artworks.

2. Students should continue independent work on their long-term multimedia and research projects.

Day 4 - Discussion of Thought Questions

1. Why do you think the inmates are compelled to gather for prayer on the eve of Rosh Hashana? What effect does this gathering have on Elie?

Time:

5 minutes

Discussion:

This scene conveys the power of ritual and tradition in the Jewish faith. The prisoners gather to observe the holiday, even in the absence of any evidence of God's presence. The high holiday ritual brings Elie's struggle with his faith into focus. In the context of the camp, the idea of the "new year" takes on a cruel irony that compounds Elie's inner turmoil.

2. What does the anecdote about Akiba Drumer suggest about Elie's own faith in God?

Time:

5 minutes

Discussion:

Elie attributes Akiba Drumer's death to his loss of faith in God. Without this, Drumer loses the will to live and submits to selection. Elie has been struggling with his own faith, questioning his devotion to a stubbornly silent God. However, this passage suggests he is still holding on to some part of his faith. Of course, Elie also has his father's well-being to consider, which motivates him to stay alive. Akiba Drumer's death is perhaps an example to Elie of what can happen when one completely abandons hope in the camps.

3. Why does another patient in the infirmary tell Elie he has "more faith in Hitler than in anyone else"? What does he mean when he says "He alone has kept his promises, all his promises, to the Jewish people"?

Time:

5 minutes

Discussion:

The other inmate's ironic comment to Elie points to the fact that Hitler has followed through, with extraordinary efficiency, on his promise to eliminate the Jews of Europe. The optimism and denial Elie witnessed in Sighet, before his family's deportation, was largely bolstered by false promises and speculation about the course of the war. Throughout his time in the camps, Elie questions how the rest of the world could go on while such atrocities are being committed against his people. It seems no one has stepped up to stop Hitler's industrial murder machine. The other inmate has clearly given up all hope in the face of brutal reality. Even with the end of the war in sight, he is more inclined to believe that Hitler will follow through on his "promise" to exterminate all the Jews in the camp than to hope for some miraculous rescue.

4. If you were in Elie's position, would you have chosen to stay in the infirmary, or left camp with the rest of the evacuees?

Time:

5 minutes

Discussion:

So many of the deaths Elie witnesses in the camps are random and utterly without logic. Making a life-and-death decision, such as whether to remain in the infirmary or evacuate the camp, is as strategic as a coin flip. Elie has no idea what choice is the right one, but still he must decide. When Wiesel writes that those who remained in the infirmary were liberated shortly after Elie's departure, the information is especially bittersweet, given the nightmarish march to Gleiwitz that comes next. Students may contemplate what information Elie had (and didn't have) to make this all-important decision, and will likely observe that either decision could easily have had dire results.

5. Why is it ironic that the *Blockälteste* makes the inmates clean the bunks one hour before the camp's evacuation?

Time:

5 minutes

Discussion:

The *Blockälteste* claims he is making the prisoners clean the bunks so the liberating army will know "that here lived men and not pigs." Wiesel notes the irony of this statement, given the constant inhumane treatment of the prisoners. Compared to the horrors perpetrated in the camp, the cleanliness of the bunks seems laughable. Clearly, the liberating army will see the crematoria and learn that the camp is a factory of death. Furthermore, the order to clean the bunks speaks to the Nazis' bureaucratic, efficient approach to genocide.

Day 4 - Short Answer Evaluation

1. On what holy day does Elie question God's will?

   _____

2. Why does Elie choose not to fast for Yom Kippur?

   _____

3. To what new Kommando do the SS assign Elie?

   _____

4. What does it mean when the SS write down the numbers of the frailest of the inmates during selection?

   _____

5. Why do the Buna "veterans" tell Elie he is lucky to have arrived when he did?

   _____

6. Why does the Blockälteste tell the prisoners to run to the inspection by SS doctors?

   _____

7. What does Akiba Drumer do that "opened the door to death"?

   _____

8. What do the prisoners eat on Christmas and New Year?

   _____

9. Why does Elie go to the infirmary?

_____

10. What was the fate of those left in the infirmary when Buna was evacuated?

_____

Answer Key

1. The eve of Rosh Hashana.
2. He wants to obey his father, who has forbidden him to fast, and he wants to rebel against God.
3. The construction Kommando.
4. That they will be sent to the crematorium.
5. Because Buna used to be much worse, with a selection every week. Two years ago, the Kapos had a weekly quota of prisoners to kill.
6. Because running will give their bodies color, making them look healthier and stronger than they are.
7. He lost his faith in God.
8. A "slightly less transparent" soup.
9. His right foot is swollen, and he needs to have an operation.
10. They were liberated by the Russians two days after the camp's evacuation.

Day 4 - Crossword Puzzle

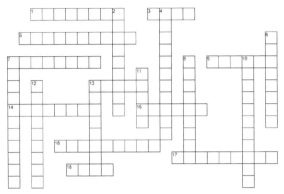

ACROSS

1. SS term for a very weak inmate
3. Elie doesn't do this on Yom Kippur
5. From this point forward
7. Severe test or trial
9. Elie's father trades this for a piece of bread
13. Elie's "inheritance," a knife and _____
14. greatness, holiness
15. Feeling or expression of sadness or regret
16. Day of Atonement (Two words)
17. For this, inmates undress to see SS doctor
18. "A veritable hell"

DOWN

2. widely known, infamous
4. Victim of selection, lost his faith in God (Two words)
6. Negotiated a trade, haggled
7. Unconditional, absolute
8. Motivation, sense of purpose
10. Religious blessing
11. Mournful sign or sound
12. Unnaturally thin, sickly
13. Characterized by grief or misfortune

Crossword Puzzle Answer Key

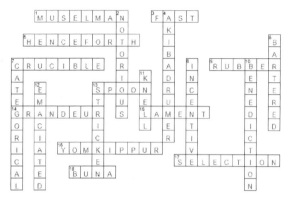

ACROSS

1. SS term for a very weak inmate
3. Elie doesn't do this on Yom Kippur
5. From this point forward
7. Severe test or trial
9. Elie's father trades this for a piece of bread
13. Elie's "inheritance," a knife and _____
14. greatness, holiness
15. Feeling or expression of sadness or regret
16. Day of Atonement (Two words)
17. For this, inmates undress to see SS doctor
18. "A veritable hell"

DOWN

2. widely known, infamous
4. Victim of selection, lost his faith in God (Two words)
6. Negotiated a trade, haggled
7. Unconditional, absolute
8. Motivation, sense of purpose
10. Religious blessing
11. Mournful sign or sound
12. Unnaturally thin, sickly
13. Characterized by grief or misfortune

Day 4 - Vocabulary Quiz

Terms

1. _____ stricken
2. _____ grandeur
3. _____ lament
4. _____ emaciated
5. _____ bartered
6. _____ plodded
7. _____ chinks
8. _____ sniggering
9. _____ categorical
10. _____ inflection

Answers

A. Cruel laughter
B. Walked slowly and with great effort
C. To feel or express sadness, mourning, or regret
D. A particular change in tone of voice
E. Characterized by grief or misfortune
F. Negotiated a trade, haggled
G. Small holes or openings
H. Greatness, impressiveness
I. Unnaturally thin
J. Unconditional, absolute

Answer Key

1. E stricken: Characterized by grief or misfortune
2. H grandeur: Greatness, impressiveness
3. C lament: To feel or express sadness, mourning, or regret
4. I emaciated: Unnaturally thin
5. F bartered: Negotiated a trade, haggled
6. B plodded: Walked slowly and with great effort
7. G chinks: Small holes or openings
8. A sniggering: Cruel laughter
9. J categorical: Unconditional, absolute
10. D inflection: A particular change in tone of voice

Day 4 - Classroom Activities

1. Kiefer and Celan: "Your Golden Hair, Margarete"

Kind of Activity:

Artistic Response

Objective:

Students will be able to comprehend Kiefer's visual response to Celan's "Death Fugue" and create original work of art based on symbols in the novel

Common Core Standards:

CCSS.ELA-LITERACY.RL.9-10.9; CCSS.ELA-LITERACY.RL.9-10.4

Time:

1 hour

Structure:

In this lesson, students will return to previous studies of poet Paul Celan and artist Anselm Kiefer to create an original artwork representing a selected scene from *Night*.

Kiefer created more than thirty works in different media based on Celan's "Death Fugue." In particular, Kiefer responded to two characters in Celan's poem: Margarete, who represents the idealized blonde Aryan woman, and Shulameth, who represents the maligned Jewish woman.

As a class, look at Kiefer's works from the 1980s titled "Your Golden Hair, Margarete." How has Kiefer responded to Celan's words in visual form? What materials and techniques does he use to represent the character of Margarete? Why would Kiefer make so many works related to Celan's poem?

Students should choose one scene, character, or symbol from *Night* to represent in a multimedia artwork. After selecting their scene, they should consider what colors, materials, and techniques to use to best represent their chosen subject. You may wish to provide a variety of art supplies and found objects (for example, old magazines and photographs, cloth, metal, wood, plastic--the less conventional, the better) to get students started. They should begin sketching and brainstorming their project in class, but should take more time outside of class to complete the work.

Ideas for Differentiated Instruction:

For students who need more support, consider providing a few suggestions of scenes, characters, or symbols to represent. Look closely at Kiefer's work and ask students to think about why he has chosen certain objects and materials to represent Margarete. Ask them to think about what associations they have with different materials, and what qualities those materials suggest. You may also want to allow additional sketching and planning time, or pair them with another student for a collaborative artwork.

For students who need a greater challenge, ask them to prepare an artist's statement describing the goals of their work.

Assessment Ideas:

Have students submit their work for assessment. Focus not on the aesthetic beauty of the finished product, but on the clarity of the ideas expressed. Does the imagery convey the selected subject? Has the student thought through the process and attempted to convey his or her ideas visually?

2. Film: Oprah and Elie Wiesel at Auschwitz

Kind of Activity:

Classwide Discussion

Objective:

Students will be able to evaluate key statements made in the filmed discussion, connecting them to broader themes in history and in the novel

Common Core Standards:

CCSS.ELA-LITERACY.SL.9-10.1.C

Time:

Time of film plus 30 minutes

Structure:

As a class, view the film "Oprah and Elie Wiesel at Auschwitz." The film is approximately 45 minutes long.

Discuss the following questions:

1. In her narration, why does Oprah refer to concentration camps as "factories of death"? When Wiesel later says, "The death factory became industrialized, and the industry worked well," what does he mean? What evidence does the film present to support this statement?

2. In his conversation with Oprah, Wiesel states, "First we were deprived of our address, then of our citizenship, then of our home, then of our family, then of our name, then of our life." How does this succinct description of the Jewish experience relate to Wiesel's narrative in *Night?* Why would the Nazis enact mass murder in this gradual fashion?

3. What does it mean to "bear witness"? Why do people continue to visit concentration camps like Auschwitz? What is Wiesel's motivation for returning to a place filled with horrible memories?

4. Wiesel says of the camp "There were trees, yes, but we didn't look." What does Wiesel mean? Why wouldn't the prisoners look at the trees?

5. Why does Wiesel describe the "individual deaths" of the inmates in Block 11 as a "privilege" in the camp?

Ideas for Differentiated Instruction:

For students who need more support, consider providing guided questions and/or a sheet scaffolding notetaking during the film.

For students who need an extra challenge, ask them to do further research the objects in the Auschwitz memorial museum.

To jumpstart the conversation, you may have students discuss the questions in pairs or small groups before moving into a full-class conversation.

Assessment Ideas:

Consider quizzing students on the historical information given in the film.

Day 5 - Reading Assignment, Questions, Vocabulary

Read from "An icy wind was blowing violently" to the end of the book, roughly 30 pages.

Common Core Objectives

- CCSS.ELA-LITERACY.RI.9-10.6
  Determine an author's point of view or purpose in a text and analyze how an author uses rhetoric to advance that point of view or purpose.

- CCSS.ELA-LITERACY.W.9-10.1
  Write arguments to support claims in an analysis of substantive topics or texts, using valid reasoning and relevant and sufficient evidence.

Note that it is perfectly fine to expand any day's work into two days depending on the characteristics of the class, particularly if the class will engage in all of the suggested classroom exercises and activities and discuss all of the thought questions.

Content Summary for Teachers

5

The march to Gleiwitz proceeds. Hundreds succumb to cold and exhaustion along the way. Some are trampled in the stampede. After walking twenty-five kilometers through the freezing night, Elie is crowded into a barrack with hundreds of other inmates. From somewhere in a pile of bodies, Elie hears Juliek the violinist calling out for help. Elie hears the sound of a violin playing the forbidden Beethoven, and later sees Juliek laying dead next to his instrument. With the Front approaching, the prisoners are loaded into cattle cars. Partway through the journey, the dead are emptied from the cars. Twenty of the one hundred people in Elie's car have died. In Germany, passersby mock the starving inmates by throwing bread into the train cars and watching them fight for it. By the time the train arrives in Buchenwald, only twelve men are left in Elie's car. At Buchenwald, Elie's father falls extremely ill with a fever and dysentery. Other prisoners beat him when he can no longer move from his bunk to relieve himself. After a week of illness and assaults by inmates and SS, Elie's father dies. Elie falls asleep in the bunk above his father, and in the morning his father is gone. On April 11, the American Army liberates Buchenwald. Elie is sent to the hospital. When he looks in the mirror for the first time since entering the camps, he sees a corpse.

Thought Questions (students consider while they read)

1. How does Zalman, the young boy from Poland, die? What does the story about Zalman's death suggest about the experience of the evacuation?

2. Why does Elie fantasize about death? What keeps him from giving in to his impulse to die?

3. After speaking with Rabbi Eliahu, who is searching for his son, Elie realizes he forgot to tell the Rabbi the he noticed the son purposefully let his father fall behind during the long run. Why is Elie glad that he has forgotten, and that the Rabbi will continue to search for his son?

4. Surrounded by dead bodies, and on the verge of death himself, why does Juliek play the violin?

5. After relating the story of a son killing his father to take his bread on the train car passing through Germany, Wiesel writes: "I was sixteen." What is the impact of these words? Why would Wiesel note his age at this point in the narrative?

Vocabulary (in order of appearance)

"We were no longer marching, we were running. Like automatons."

automatons:

Mechanical figures that move by their own power, robots

Unthinking mechanical beings

"We had transcended everything--death, fatigue, our natural needs."

transcended :

Extended beyond

"How had he succeeded in disengaging himself?"

disengaging:

Removing from action or involvement

"Our minds numb with indifference."

indifference:

Lack of concern or caring

"Men were hurling themselves against each other, trampling, tearing at and mauling each other."

mauling:

Violently attacking in order to injure or damage

"An extraordinary vitality possessed them, sharpening their teeth and nails."

vitality :

Life force, energy

"His eyes lit up, a smile, like a grimace, illuminated his ashen face."

grimace:

A facial expression of pain or displeasure, often ugly or menacing

"He dragged me toward a pile of snow from which protruded human shapes, torn blankets."

protruded:

Stuck out, projected

Additional Homework

1. Complete Kiefer-inspired artwork.

2. Finalize long-term project for submission, taking notes from the classroom presentation into account.

Day 5 - Discussion of Thought Questions

1. How does Zalman, the young boy from Poland, die? What does the story about Zalman's death suggest about the experience of the evacuation?

Time:

5 minutes

Discussion:

Zalman dies in an embarrassing way--literally with his pants down. He is overcome by gastrointestinal distress, and falls to the ground in an attempt to relieve his bowels. With this story, Wiesel conveys the inhumanity of the evacuation. Men die without a shred of dignity. Furthermore, Wiesel believes Zalman was trampeled by the other inmates, rather than shot by the SS. The men are moving unthinkingly, both fueled and numbed by fear. There is little opportunity to comfort one another, and no chance to help a fallen comrade. If one wants to survive, one must keep moving, even if it means leaving a friend behind to die.

2. Why does Elie fantasize about death? What keeps him from giving in to his impulse to die?

Time:

5 minutes

Discussion:

On the long run in the snow during the evacuation, Elie begins to think of death as a relief from the pains of existence. He is running on his wounded foot, in extreme pain, and imagines death will be swift. The knowledge that his father is still alive and running next to him is what keeps him going. He feels responsible for his father's fate.

3. After speaking with Rabbi Eliahu, who is searching for his son, Elie realizes he forgot to tell the Rabbi the he noticed the son purposefully let his father fall behind during the long run. Why is Elie glad that he has forgotten, and that the Rabbi will continue to search for his son?

Time:

5 minutes

Discussion:

Perhaps Elie believes that searching for his son will give the Rabbi hope and purpose, and will thus help him stay alive. Elie's attachment to his own father is largely what has kept him alive to this point. Elie may also be glad that he spared the Rabbi from the harsh truth that his son abandoned him. In these conditions, it is likely that both the Rabbi and his son will end up dead; at this point, it may be simply cruel to let the Rabbi know the truth.

4. Surrounded by dead bodies, and on the verge of death himself, why does Juliek play the violin?

Time:

5 minutes

Discussion:

Students should consider the power of passions. Even in the most dire circumstance, Juliek was compelled to play--and hear--his beloved violin one more time. Students may speculate that music was the most important thing in Juliek's life before the concentration camps, and that his final act was a way of reclaiming that former self. It is important to note that he plays Beethoven, which he was forbidden to play in the camps. This may be thought of as a final act of defiance against those who caused Juliek's death (and the deaths of so many others).

5. After relating the story of a son killing his father to take his bread on the train car passing through Germany, Wiesel writes: "I was sixteen." What is the impact of these words? Why would Wiesel note his age at this point in the narrative?

Time:

5 minutes

Discussion:

The story of the son killing his father, and then being killed himself by other starving inmates, represents a new level of the prisoners' inhumanity. They have been starved for several days while in transit, and alleviating hunger has finally overcome all other considerations. Students might connect this episode to the previous story of Rabbi Eliahu's son leaving his aging father behind on the march. When prisoners reach points of desperation, even the bonds of family cease to matter. When he concludes this particular passage with "I was sixteen," Elie points to the complete corruption of his youthful innocence. By this young age, he has witnessed the heights of cruelty and despair. In three years, he has experienced the darkest reaches of human behavior. Several times, he has nearly lost the will to live. His father has been his ultimate reason to survive. Here, he juxtaposes a scene of debased violence with a reminder of his own humanity--his youth.

Day 5 - Short Answer Evaluation

1. How was the Polish man named Zalman most likely killed?

   _____

2. About how far had the inmates been run when they reached the abandoned village?

   _____

3. Where do Elie and his father seek shelter in the village?

   _____

4. What warning does Elie's father give him inside the brick factory?

   _____

5. Who is Rabbi Eliahu searching for?

   _____

6. What does Elie forget to tell Rabbi Eliahu?

   _____

7. What does Elie ask for in his prayer?

   _____

8. In what location does the long march end?

   _____

9. Who does Elie hear crying for mercy in a pile of bodies?

10. How does Elie find out his father has died?

Answer Key

1. He was probably trampled.
2. Twenty kilometers.
3. In an abandoned brick factory.
4. He warns Elie not to fall asleep in the snow; he tells him he will die if he falls asleep.
5. His son.
6. That he had seen the Rabbi's son running next to him.
7. He asks for the strength not to abandon his father, as Rabbi Eliahu's son had done.
8. In Gleiwitz.
9. Juliek, the Warsaw violinist.
10. When he goes to his father's cot, there is another man lying there.

Day 5 - Crossword Puzzle

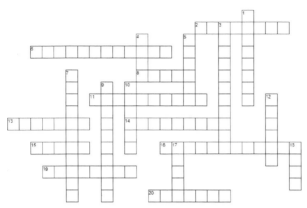

ACROSS

2. life force, energy
6. lack of concern or caring
8. "On April 5, the _____ of history turned."
11. Unthinking mechanical figures
13. violently attacking
14. stuck out, projecting
15. In Germany, someone throws this in the train car
16. They throw the dead from the train
19. Elie's fathers friend, a gardener (Two words)
20. Expression of pain or displeasure

DOWN

1. After the long march, Elie stays here for three days
3. extended beyond
4. With no food, the prisoners eat this
5. In the darkness, Elie hears only this
7. removing from action or involvement
9. Concentration camp where Elie's father dies
10. What Elie sees in the mirror
12. Violinist from Warsaw
17. _____ Eliahu
18. Elie dreams of this

Crossword Puzzle Answer Key

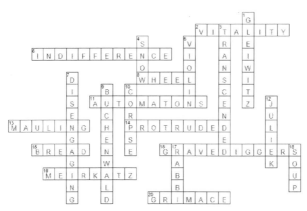

ACROSS
2. life force, energy
6. lack of concern or caring
8. "On April 5, the _____ of history turned."
11. Unthinking mechanical figures
13. violently attacking
14. stuck out, projecting
15. In Germany, someone throws this in the train car
16. They throw the dead from the train
19. Elie's fathers friend, a gardener (Two words)
20. Expression of pain or displeasure

DOWN
1. After the long march, Elie stays here for three days
3. extended beyond
4. With no food, the prisoners eat this
5. In the darkness, Elie hears only this
7. removing from action or involvement
9. Concentration camp where Elie's father dies
10. What Elie sees in the mirror
12. Violinist from Warsaw
17. _____ Eliahu
18. Elie dreams of this

Day 5 - Vocabulary Quiz

Terms

1. _____ automatons
2. _____ transcended
3. _____ disengaging
4. _____ indifference
5. _____ mauling
6. _____ vitality
7. _____ grimace
8. _____ protruded

Answers

A. Lack of concern or caring
B. Facial expression of pain or displeasure
C. Violently attacking in order to injure or damage
D. Stuck out, projected
E. Extended beyond
F. Unthinking mechanical beings
G. Life force, energy
H. Removing from action or involvement

Answer Key

1. F automatons: Unthinking mechanical beings
2. E transcended: Extended beyond
3. H disengaging: Removing from action or involvement
4. A indifference: Lack of concern or caring
5. C mauling: Violently attacking in order to injure or damage
6. G vitality: Life force, energy
7. B grimace: Facial expression of pain or displeasure
8. D protruded: Stuck out, projected

Day 5 - Classroom Activities

1. 'Night' as Art: A Debate

Kind of Activity:

Classwide Discussion

Objective:

Students will be able to evaluate Night as a work of art, and the affect of time on perceptions of history

Common Core Standards:

CCSS.ELA-LITERACY.RI.9-10.6

Time:

40 minutes

Structure:

Have students read silently the 1964 article "The Literature of the Holocaust" by A. Alvarez, published in *Commentary Magazine*. Instruct them to read closely, noting questions, and underlining important sentences and unfamiliar words.

You can find the article here: http://www.commentarymagazine.com/article/the-literature-of-the-holocaust/

As a class, have a volunteer read aloud the paragraph that begins "As a human document, *Night* is almost unbearably painful, and certainly beyond criticism." Here, Alvarez claims that *Night* "is a failure as a work of art." Ask students to consider Alvarez's criteria for a work of art. What reasons does he give for making this claim? Does the passage he cites as an example effectively support his argument that the novel is a failure as a work of art?

Ask students to consider their own criteria for identifying a work of art. Must art be beautiful? Is it possible to make art out of a tragedy as severe as the Holocaust?

Writing in 1964, Alvarez comments that, in the twenty years' time since the Holocaust, the meaning of the events has "changed slightly." How does time impact how we view tragic events in history and in our own lives? Did you have an emotional response to the novel? Do you feel any personal connection to the Holocaust, or does it have any special significance in your life?

To tie these themes to more contemporary events, you might ask your students how old they were on Sept. 11, 2001. What do they know about the 9/11 attacks? Have they heard personal stories from their parents, relatives, or friends about these events? What do they think people will remember or feel about 9/11 in fifty years? Is it possible that *Night* was not a work of art when Alvarez was writing, but is now?

Ideas for Differentiated Instruction:

For students who need more support, consider providing the article and discussion questions in advance as homework.

Assessment Ideas:

Have students submit a short written response to one of the in-class discussion questions.

2. Elie Wiesel Nobel Prize Acceptance Speech

Kind of Activity:

Individual Writing

Objective:

Students will be able to identify and interpret main arguments presented in Wiesel's speech

Common Core Standards:

CCSS.ELA-LITERACY.W.9-10.1

Time:

Time of video plus 20 minutes

Structure:

As a class, watch video of Elie Wiesel's 1986 Nobel Prize acceptance speech. The video, which is 18 minutes long, can be found at nobelprize.org: http://www.nobelprize.org/mediaplayer/index.php?id=2028

After watching the video, have students respond individually in writing to the following prompts:

1. What are the main arguments Wiesel makes in his speech?

2. In his speech, Wiesel says, "If we forget, we are guilty. ... If we forget them, they will be killed a second time." What does Wiesel mean here? Why is it important to remember the Holocaust?

Ideas for Differentiated Instruction:

For students who need extra support, consider allowing extra time to compose a response. You might also consider giving them the option of writing a first draft focused on the clear expression of ideas, and a second draft focused on correct spelling, grammar, formatting, etc.

Consider giving students an option of typing or writing by hand, or of utilizing text-to-speech software.

For students who need a greater challenge, ask them to consider the purpose of the Nobel Prize, as well as the purpose of a Nobel Prize speech.

Assessment Ideas:

Have students turn in their written responses for assessment.

3. Presentation of Long-Term Projects

Kind of Activity:

Long-term Project

Objective:

Students will be able to showcase their work and evaluate one another's projects

Time:

30 minutes

Structure:

Students should choose to present one of their projects, either their piece of genocide research or their multimedia timelines.

Organize the class so that several students are simultaneously presenting their projects to small groups of other students. Each person should have about five minutes to present their work and to answer questions from teachers and students about their research and discoveries.

While observing their classmates, students should consider the following questions:

-What are the strongest aspects of this project?

-Have you learned anything from your classmate's work that you did not know before? If so, what have you learned, and why do you consider it significant?

-How does this project relate to the research that you yourself conducted?

After seeing a range of student projects, students should write up the answers to these questions and turn them in for evaluation. If you so choose, you can share student feedback with the presenters.

Ideas for Differentiated Instruction:

The public speaking component of the exercise could be eliminated, with students simply interacting with one another's timelines or written research in their intended forms.

Assessment Ideas:

Students should be assessed on their participation and the strength of their observations.

Final Paper

Essay Questions

1. Analyze Elie's relationship with his father throughout the book. When and how does the relationship benefit each of them, and, alternately, hinder them? Also consider the broader theme of father/son relationships in the book.

2. Analyze the role of religion in the novel. How does belief in God help or hurt Elie and those around him? How does faith impact Elie's and other prisoners' experience/s in the concentration camps?

3. Evaluate the significance of the novel's title with regards to the narrative. What does night symbolize in the book?

4. Discuss the relationship between dehumanization and human kindness in the novel. By what means and methods do the Nazis dehumanize the camp prisoners? How do the prisoners treat one another? In what ways are the prisoners complicit in this process of dehumanization? What moments of humanity does Wiesel describe, and what is their significance?

5. Compare Wiesel's narrative with another representation of the Holocaust, either literary or visual. How do both artists articulate the experience of the concentration camps? What are the similarities and differences between their interpretations?

6. Evaluate the statement made by critic A. Alvarez, that "'Night' is 'beyond criticism' as a 'human document,' but 'a failure as a work of art.' Wiesel, he argued, had failed to 'create a coherent artistic world out of one which was the deliberate negation of all values.'" What does he mean by this statement, and how would you respond to it?

7. Discuss the relationship between silence and sound in the book. What does silence signify? What sounds stand out in the narrative, and why are they important?

Advice on research sources

A. School or community library

Ask your reference librarian for help locating books on the following subjects:

*Elie Wiesel

*World War II in Europe

*The Holocaust (historical and literary texts)

*Genocide

*Judaism

B. Personal interviews

*Ask people who lived through World War II to describe their memories of learning about the liberation of the concentration camps, or speak to their immediate descendents about their parents' experiences and memories

C. Other works

Consider related narratives of the Holocaust, including Livia Bitton-Jackson's *I Have Lived a Thousand Years* and Wladyslaw Szpilman's *The Pianist.*

Grading rubric for essays

Style:

* words: spelling and diction

* sentences: grammar and punctuation

* paragraphs: organization

* essay: structure

* argument: rhetoric, reasonableness, creativity

Content:

* accuracy

* use of evidence

* addressing of the question

* completeness

* use of literary concepts

Answer Key for Final Essays

Remember that essays about literature should not be graded with a cookie-cutter approach whereby specific words or ideas are required. See the grading rubric above for a variety of criteria to use in assessing answers to the essay questions. This answer key thus functions as a store of ideas for students who need additional guidance in framing their answers.

1. Analyze Elie's relationship with his father throughout the book. When and how does the relationship benefit each of them, and, alternately, hinder them? Also consider the broader theme of father/son relationships in the book.

Strong answers will make a clear, specific argument weighing the importance of Elie's relationship with his father to the survival of both men. They will also consider moments when Elie's attachment to his father challenges his own survival, and consider how these difficulties affect Elie's conception of himself. They should also include some consideration of other fathers and sons, such as Rabbi Eliahu and the son who abandons him.

2. Analyze the role of religion in the novel. How does belief in God help or hurt Elie and those around him? How does faith impact Elie's and other prisoners' experience/s in the concentration camps?

The Jewish victims of the Holocaust were persecuted based on their religion; students should analyze the ways that Jews maintained their faith and questioned it in this context. Essays should address the ways in which Elie's faith defines his character, especially at the beginning of the novel. They will draw from several scenes in which Elie questions his own faith. Furthermore, they will cite passages in which Elie describes other characters' reliance on, or defiance of, religion.

3. Evaluate the significance of the novel's title with regards to the narrative. What does night symbolize in the book?

Essays should closely consider the novel's figurative language, making a clear argument about the symbolic meaning of the novel's title. Students should perform close readings of passages that deploy night as a symbol to illustrate larger ideas. They should consider how the experiences of deportation and camp life challenge

Elie's notion of time and of himself. They should also consider how these experiences came to haunt the rest of the author's life after liberation.

4. Discuss the relationship between dehumanization and human kindness in the novel. By what means and methods do the Nazis dehumanize the camp prisoners? How do the prisoners treat one another? In what ways are the prisoners complicit in this process of dehumanization? What moments of humanity does Wiesel describe, and what is their significance?

Strong answers will draw on specific examples from the text to characterize the Nazi strategies for dehumanizing Jewish subjects. They will also cite passages that describe cruel acts and behaviors between prisoners, and analyze the reasons for them. Furthermore, they will provide counterpoints for this evidence, citing significant passages describing particular acts of kindness and analyzing how these impact the overall narrative. Some students may believe that the level of dehumanization that the victims suffered brought them to a place of greater human kindness and understanding; others may see the triumph of dehumanization in the context of the book.

5. Compare Wiesel's narrative with another representation of the Holocaust, either literary or visual. How do both artists articulate the experience of the concentration camps? What are the similarities and differences between their interpretations?

Strong answers will specifically address the characteristics of different media and how each representational mode conveys its subject matter. They will make a clear argument based on a comparison of both modes of representation, drawing specific examples from each. They will also make larger claims about the nature of each representation, considering how each engages the reader/viewer.

6. Evaluate the statement made by critic A. Alvarez, that "'Night' is 'beyond criticism' as a 'human document,' but 'a failure as a work of art.' Wiesel, he argued, had failed to 'create a coherent artistic world out of one which was the deliberate negation of all values.'" What does he

mean by this statement, and how would you respond to it?

Strong answers will perform close readings of the text, focusing on figurative and symbolic language and how Wiesel utilizes such devices to articulate his subject matter. They will make a strong claim either in support of Alvarez's statement, or in defense of the novel. These answers will also clearly articulate a position relative to the definition of art, and explain how the novel either does or does not satisfy the criteria of art.

7. Discuss the relationship between silence and sound in the book. What does silence signify? What sounds stand out in the narrative, and why are they important?

Students should consider the symbolic meanings of silence--particularly Wiesel's feeling that God has abandoned him and the other prisoners to the camps--and compare and contrast this evidence with the meaning of particular sounds throughout the novel. The essays will most likely contain a discussion of music in the novel, considering how music is used in the camps to regulate the prisoners. Furthermore, they will analyze the character Juliek, and analyze the final scene in which Elie hears Juliek playing his violin for the last time.

Final Exam

Multiple Choice

Circle the letter corresponding to the best answer.

1. What is Elie's full first name?

    A. Eliezer
    B. Eliahu
    C. Elias
    D. Elazar

2. Who taught Elie the Kabbalah?

    A. His father
    B. Moishe the Beadle
    C. Batia Reich
    D. Moishe Chaim Berkowitz

3. During what season is Elie's family deported from Sighet?

    A. Winter
    B. Spring
    C. Summer
    D. Autumn

4. What are the names of Elie's three sisters?

    A. Bea, Hilda, and Rachel
    B. Tzipora, Bea, and Hilda
    C. Tzipora, Ágota, and Dorottya
    D. Tzipora, Rivka,and Elisheva

5. What form of Judaism does Elie's family follow?

    A. Ashkenazic
    B. Sephardic
    C. Reform
    D. Hasidic

6. When did Elie ask his father to buy emigration certificates to Palestine?

A. Winter 1943
B. Summer 1944
C. Spring 1944
D. Spring 1943

7. What was the people of Sighet's first impression of the German soldiers?

A. They were violent and cruel
B. They were cruel, but seemed remorseful
C. They were distant, but polite
D. They were very friendly

8. What symbol were the Jews of Sighet forced to wear?

A. Red "J"
B. Blue star
C. Yellow cross
D. Yellow star

9. What does Maria, the Wiesels' former maid, beg them to do?

A. To give her money to pay for emigration papers
B. To go with her to her village where she has prepared safe shelter
C. To let her stay in their house
D. To help her flee Sighet

10. What does the German officer demand of the prisoners during their stop in Kaschau?

A. Their identification papers
B. One hundred push-ups each
C. Their clothes
D. Their gold, silver, and watches

11. Who was traveling with Mrs. Schächter?

A. Her ten-year-old son

B. Her fourteen-year-old daughter and ten-year-old son
C. Her husband and three sons
D. She was traveling alone

12. At what time does Elie's transport arrive in Birkenau?

A. Around midnight
B. Dawn
C. Around sunset
D. Between three and four in the morning

13. What occupation does Elie claim in his interview with Dr. Mengele?

A. Farmer
B. Electrician
C. Student
D. Teacher

14. What does the Sonder-Kommando do?

A. Work as personal assistants to the SS
B. Work in the electronics factory
C. Work in the crematoria
D. Hard labor in the construction yard

15. Which of the following does not happen Elie the first night at Birkenau?

A. He is beaten by Kapos
B. He is shaved at the barber
C. He has a gold crown removed
D. He is stripped naked

16. What relative does Elie see in Auschwitz?

A. His schoolmate Ezra Malik
B. Stein, his Aunt Reizel's husband
C. His Aunt Reizel
D. His Uncle Mendel

17. How long do Elie and his father stay at Auschwitz?

A. Three weeks
B. One month
C. Four months
D. Two days

18. Who is the foreman of the camp orchestra?

A. Juliek
B. Idek
C. Franek
D. Louis

19. What "beautiful present" does the SS give the inmates for the new year?

A. Extra soup
B. A public execution
C. Selection
D. A forced march

20. What is the prisoners' "first act as free men"?

A. They weep
B. They eat
C. They thank the American soldiers
D. They sleep

Short Answer

1. Who wrote the last piece of music Juliek plays on his violin?

   _____

2. Where does Elie's father die?

   _____

3. How many siblings does Elie have?

   _____

4. How is Elie's gold crown removed?

   _____

5. What does Elie's father give him when he thinks he has been "selected"?

   _____

6. When is Buchenwald liberated?

   _____

7. What happens to the personal belongings the deportees brought with them on the train to Poland?

   _____

8. When does Elie see his mother and Tzipora for the last time?

   _____

9. How does Idek the Kapo punish Elie after Elie catches Idek having sex with a young Polish girl?

10. What does Elie see when he looks at himself in the mirror after the liberation of Buchenwald?

Vocabulary Questions

Terms

1. _____ shtibl
2. _____ Kabbalah
3. _____ surreptitiously
4. _____ insinuated
5. _____ billeted
6. _____ harangued
7. _____ veritable
8. _____ manacled
9. _____ emaciated
10. _____ mauling
11. _____ automatons
12. _____ indifference
13. _____ categorical
14. _____ lament
15. _____ pittance
16. _____ sanctity
17. _____ invectives
18. _____ imperative
19. _____ synagogue
20. _____ disquieting

Answers

A. Upsetting, unsettling
B. A small amount
C. To feel or express sadness, mourning, or regret
D. Unnaturally thin
E. Unthinking mechanical beings
F. Yiddish: A small house of prayer for the Hasidic sect of the Jewish faith
G. Secretly, stealthily
H. True, utter
I. A Jewish house of worship
J. Yelled at, verbally assaulted
K. Absolutely necessary
L. Unconditional, absolute
M. Suggested, implied
N. An ancient, mystical tradition in Judaism
O. Harsh and contemptuous insults, accusations
P. Violently attacking in order to injure or damage
Q. Holiness, sacredness
R. Temporarily stationed, lodged
S. Lack of concern or caring
T. Shackled, handcuffed

Short Essays

1. In section 1, Elie quotes his father as saying "The yellow star? So what? It's not lethal...", to which Elie rhetorically replies, "(Poor Father! Of what then did you die?)" Explain and analyze Elie's statement.

_____

_____

_____

_____

2. What is the nature of Elie's relationship with Moishe the Beadle?

_____

_____

_____

_____

_____

3. How does hunger impact Elie's feelings and behavior in the novel?

_____

_____

_____

_____

4. How does Elie react to the deaths he witnesses in the camps, and why? Are there any deaths that affect him more than others?

_____

_____

_____

_____

_____

Final Exam Answer Key

Multiple Choice

1. **(A)** Eliezer
2. **(B)** Moishe the Beadle
3. **(C)** Summer
4. **(B)** Tzipora, Bea, and Hilda
5. **(D)** Hasidic
6. **(C)** Spring 1944
7. **(C)** They were distant, but polite
8. **(D)** Yellow star
9. **(B)** To go with her to her village where she has prepared safe shelter
10. **(D)** Their gold, silver, and watches
11. **(A)** Her ten-year-old son
12. **(A)** Around midnight
13. **(A)** Farmer
14. **(C)** Work in the crematoria
15. **(C)** He has a gold crown removed
16. **(B)** Stein, his Aunt Reizel's husband
17. **(A)** Three weeks
18. **(C)** Franek
19. **(C)** Selection
20. **(B)** They eat

Short Answer

1. Beethoven.
2. In Buchenwald.
3. He has three sisters.
4. With a rusty spoon in the camp latrine.
5. A knife and a spoon.
6. April 1945.
7. All belongings are left behind in the train cars.
8. Immediately after arriving at Birkenau, when the men and women are separated.
9. He gives Elie twenty-five lashes in public.
10. A corpse.

Vocabulary Questions

1. F shtibl: Yiddish: A small house of prayer for the Hasidic sect of the Jewish faith
2. N Kabbalah: An ancient, mystical tradition in Judaism
3. G surreptitiously : Secretly, stealthily
4. M insinuated: Suggested, implied
5. R billeted: Temporarily stationed, lodged
6. J harangued : Yelled at, verbally assaulted
7. H veritable: True, utter
8. T manacled: Shackled, handcuffed
9. D emaciated: Unnaturally thin
10. P mauling: Violently attacking in order to injure or damage
11. E automatons: Unthinking mechanical beings
12. S indifference: Lack of concern or caring
13. L categorical: Unconditional, absolute
14. C lament: To feel or express sadness, mourning, or regret
15. B pittance: A small amount
16. Q sanctity: Holiness, sacredness
17. O invectives: Harsh and contemptuous insults, accusations
18. K imperative: Absolutely necessary
19. I synagogue: A Jewish house of worship
20. A disquieting: Upsetting, unsettling

Short Essays

1. In part, Elie's statment suggests that, retrospectively, he believes that the gradual process of relinquishing rights ultimately led to the extermination of the Jews in the concentration camps. Being forced to wear a yellow star while still living in Sighet is one of these "small" offenses that, when combined, resulted in mass killing. Furthermore, the star is a symbol of Judaism. Being forced to wear the star marked one as a Jew, for easy identification by the Nazis. Elie's statement also speaks to the fact that the hatred of the Jews fueled the Nazi's elaborate plot of extermination. Wearing the star itself was not lethal, but what it symbolized certainly was.

2. Moishe the Beadle was a kind of spiritual guide to the young Elie, who was extremely curious about and invested in his religion. His father would not help him find a master to study the Kabbalah, and Moishe the Beadle became an unlikely guide in the place of a formal teacher. Looking back, this figure takes on even more significance for Elie because Moishe was the first to warn the Jews of Sighet of the Nazi atrocities.

3. The hunger Elie experiences in the camps changes him physically, mentally, and spiritually. His extreme hunger dominates his thoughts, and dulls his moral compass. Because he is starving, he becomes even more desensitized to the atrocities around him. At the end of the novel, he does not even recognize himself in the mirror--but this change into a "corpse" is emotional as well as physical. What he has experienced has brough him close to death in many ways.

4. As the novel progresses, Elie becomes increasingly desensitized to the deaths he witnesses. During the long march to Gleiwitz and again in the train ride through Germany near the end of the novel, men are constantly dying all around him. He writes that he has witnessed many public hangings, but the one that most affects him is the hanging of the kind *pipel*, the young boy who does not weigh enough to die instantaneously at the gallows. This execution, of a child, has the greatest impact on Elie's consciousness. This scene recalls a moment when he first arrives at Auschwitz and is struck by the mass burning of small children and babies.

GradeSaver™

Getting you the grade since 1999™

Other Lesson Plans from GradeSaver™

12 Angry Men
1984
A Doll's House
Alice in Wonderland
Animal Farm
An Inspector Calls
Antigone
A Streetcar Named
    Desire
A Thousand
    Splendid Suns
Atonement
Beowulf
Brave New World
Death of a Salesman
Do Androids Dream
    of Electric Sheep?
Emily Dickinson's
    Collected Poems
Everyman: Morality
    Play
Fahrenheit 451

Flannery O'Connor's
    Stories
Great Expectations
Gulliver's Travels
Hamlet
Heart of Darkness
In Cold Blood
In the Time of the
    Butterflies
Into the Wild
Jane Eyre
John Donne: Poems
Kate Chopin's Short
    Stories
Leaves of Grass
Life of Pi
Lord of the Flies
Macbeth
MAUS
Never Let Me Go
Night
Oedipus Rex or
    Oedipus the King

Of Mice and Men
Oliver Twist
One Flew Over the
    Cuckoo's Nest
Oryx and Crake
Othello
Persepolis: The
    Story of a
    Childhood
Poe's Poetry
Pride and Prejudice
Robert Frost: Poems
Robinson Crusoe
Roll of Thunder,
    Hear My Cry
Romeo and Juliet
Shakespeare's
    Sonnets
Songs of Innocence
    and of Experience
The Adventures of
    Huckleberry Finn

For our full list of over 300 Study Guides, Quizzes, Lesson Plans
Sample College Application Essays, Literature Essays and E-texts, visit:

www.gradesaver.com

Lesson Plans

Gr deSaver™

Getting you the grade since 1999™

Other Lesson Plans from GradeSaver™

The Alchemist
   (Coelho)
The Bloody
   Chamber
The Book Thief
The Brief Wondrous
   Life of Oscar Wao
The Canterbury
   Tales
The Catcher in the
   Rye
The Count of Monte
   Cristo
The Crucible
The Curious
   Incident of the

Dog in the Night-
   time
The Diary of a
   Young Girl by
   Anne Frank
The God of Small
   Things
The Great Gatsby
The Hobbit
The Kite Runner
The Odyssey
The Old Man and
   the Sea
The Outsiders
The Road
The Scarlet Letter

The Tortilla Curtain
The Yellow
   Wallpaper
To Build a Fire
To Kill a
   Mockingbird
Trifles
Wordsworth's
   Poetical Works
Wuthering Heights
Young Goodman
   Brown and Other
   Hawthorne Short
   Stories

For our full list of over 300 Study Guides, Quizzes, Lesson Plans
Sample College Application Essays, Literature Essays and E-texts, visit:

www.gradesaver.com

Made in the USA
San Bernardino, CA
29 September 2018